AMERICA'S BEST COLLEGES!
REALLY?

JOHN A. HOWARD

CROSSBOOKS
PUBLISHING

CrossBooks™
A Division of LifeWay
1663 Liberty Drive
Bloomington, IN 47403
www.crossbooks.com
Phone: 1-866-879-0502

First published by CrossBooks 06/11/2012

ISBN: 978-1-4627-1831-3 (sc)
ISBN: 978-1-4627-1833-7 (hc)
ISBN: 978-1-4627-1832-0 (e)

Library of Congress Control Number: 2012908253

Printed in the United States of America

This book is printed on acid-free paper.

DEDICATION TO

Angus MacDonald
Founding (1967) Editor of
The Saint Croix Review
Stillwater, Minnesota

And

James Crawford
Founding (1986) Editor of
The Herald Examiner
Freeville, New York

These two monthly periodicals have consistently presented speeches, articles and essays elucidating the fundamental wisdom required for America's Free Society

PREFACE

Annually, two well-regarded magazines have published their lists of America's Best Colleges. This is a service they provide to assist students in determining which college to attend. The colleges are so numerous, the cost so high, and the college experience so pivotal in influencing the student's life that advice from a respected resource is warmly welcomed by students and their families.

In its 2010 update, Forbes explains "We rank undergraduate institutions on the quality of education they provide, the experience of their students, and how much their graduates achieve . . . . Every school with a Forbes grade meets a high standard." A high standard of what?

U.S. News and World Report explains that its 2010 judgment of the "Best Colleges" takes into account "a variety of factors that measure academic quality, from student selectivity to faculty resources to peer assessment. We talk to students, parents and educators. We crunch the numbers, we evaluate how the schools stack up, then we present the results in charts, lists and stories." How the schools stack up with regard to what?

One has to assume that the best colleges have an especially good program of education, but there isn't a clue in either statement about the educational philosophy undergirding the educational program which leads to a high rating. Years ago there was an entertainer who would speak at large conferences. He was billed as "Professor Irwin Corey, The World's Foremost Expert." He would have the program chairman provide him with a short speech pertinent to the conference. As he read it, from time to time he would insert a word of complete gibberish and move on without missing a beat. And do it again. And again. If the audience didn't catch on, after a while he would lapse into utter nonsense. Professor Corey comes to mind in reading the explanations of the rating systems.

The two magazines cannot be blamed for this fiasco. They have been blind-sided by the complete inversion of the meaning and the purpose of education that began in the early decades of the twentieth century and progressed until it erupted in mind-boggling turmoil in the mid-nineteen-sixties. The nation-wide student rampage involved the take-over of college buildings, spraying walls with graffiti, throwing bricks through plate glass windows, stealing or damaging professors' research, shouting down guest speakers, and at the University of Wisconsin, bombing a college building and killing a professor inside. When the turmoil subsided, America breathed a sigh of relief that the student high-jinks had run its course, but people did not have any idea of the educational transformation that had contributed to the campus chaos and accounted for the generally feeble attempts to control it.

Aristotle wrote:

> Of all the things I have mentioned, that which contributes most to the permanence of constitutions is the adaption of education to the form of government.

With the exceptions of religion and the family, schooling is the foremost determinant of the well-being of a nation. Even with the wisest leadership, it is the bedrock character of the citizens that will decide whether America can find its way honorably and successfully through the confusion and the contention and the doubt that now hold America in their grip. The quality of a nation's educational system is reflected not only in the citizens' knowledge and technical skills, but also in the principles that guide their conduct and the priorities they insist upon. These are the factors which ultimately will tip the balance toward the renewed strength or the further deterioration of our society.

In 1748, a book by French political philosopher, Charles Montesquieu, was published. It was entitled The Spirit of the Laws. It analyzed various forms of government. Montesquieu stated that each one had a unique relationship with the people, and if that relationship changed, that form of government would perish. In a despotism or tyranny, the government could last as long as the people were afraid of it, doing what they were told to do for fear of severe penalties.

A monarchy could last as long as the people were loyal to the crown.

A democracy, or other self-governing regime, depended upon a virtuous populace which voluntarily abided by the laws and other settled standards of behavior. This free society was the best form of government, and the hardest to achieve and sustain. America's free society was destined for success because the colonists who came to New England had left England for the sole purpose of finding a land where they could practice their Christian faith free of governmental intervention and persecution. Their lives were dedicated to fulfilling their Christian faith. These people were already deeply committed to a virtuous life, wholly suited for the government of a free society.

The Founding Fathers of America fully understood and supported the cardinal principle proclaimed by Aristotle. On July 17, 1787, the Continental Congress enacted the Northwest Ordinance. It set forth the plan for the government of the residents of the Northwest Territory and the basis on which a region might qualify for statehood. Article III begins, "Religion, morality and knowledge being necessary to good government and the happiness of mankind, schools and the means of education shall be forever encouraged." Here is an acknowledgment that our self-government is dependent on religion, morality and education in that order of importance. That document and The Declaration of Independence, and the United States Constitution were so intelligently conceived that they reflect a breadth of knowledge and wisdom often said to be superior to the products of any other deliberative body in world history. Certainly, there have been no comparable accomplishments in recent times.

Buckminster Fuller, America's all-purpose genius, once provided an explanation of the diminishing frequency of truly brilliant analytical thinking in America nowadays. The occasion was a very large conference. As then President of Rockford College, I had given a speech about education. Fuller lumbered up to the podium and stood there silently for a bit. He then said, "Before I give my talk, I want to say something to that fellow who just finished. You folks in the colleges are going to be the ruination of this country. What you do is single out the brightest students as they come through and make them experts in something. That isn't all bad, but it leaves a residue of mediocre minds and dunderheads to become the generalists needed to serve as college presidents." When the laughter subsided, he said, "And the presidents of the United States!!!"

A competent generalist understands human nature, is familiar with the social and political institutions of the country, their interdependence and vulnerability, and the principles which govern what they can and cannot do. As a result, he is more likely than others to be able to anticipate the consequences of his judgments for his own organization and for the society. Today, there are precious few generalists in positions of authority in any field of endeavor, which undoubtedly explains why the social institutions don't work very well any more.

Back through history it has been understood that the core of a nation's educational program is the training of each new generation so that they will know about, and embrace the ideals and values and virtues of the society, informing the students why those values are of prime importance, what the obligations are that each individual must accept and the taboos each must observe in order for those values to be sustained. The young are taught about the heroes who sacrificed greatly to protect and defend the values, and the scoundrels who defied and tried to subvert them. This acculturation was not perceived as a difficult and oppressive requirement because the society generally lived according to the values so that learning the individual responsibilities was like learning to speak the language.

This concept of the primary role of education served all societies, primitive as well as advanced, Marxist as well as self-governing. It animated the schooling of the first colonies and continued on through the development of the American nation.

The stress on religion and morality in the Northwest Ordinance was echoed in the main body of George Washington's Inaugural Address two years later. American education's faithful attention to the development of character among the students was summarized in a 1979 Report published by The Hastings Center. The author was Columbia Professor Douglas Sloan. He wrote:

> Throughout most of the 19th Century the most important course in the college curriculum was moral philosophy, taught usually by the college president and required of all senior students . . .
>
> The full significance and centrality of moral philosophy in the 19th Century college curriculum can only be understood in the light of the assumption held by American leaders and most ordinary citizens that no nation could survive, let alone prosper, without some common moral and social values . . .
>
> However moral philosophy did not carry the whole burden of forming the students' character and guiding their conduct; the entire college experience was meant above all to be an experience in character development and the moral life. [1]

During the 20th Century, a number of factors contributed to the radicalization of education.

1. Impact of New Ideologies.

In 1848, Marx and Engels published The Communist Manifesto which provided an impetus and a manual for radical social change. The Industrial Revolution, powered by capitalism, an anathema to Communism, produced innumerable factories employing thousands of people whose work had been virtually eliminated by machines and mass production. Often the wages and working conditions were deplorable. In the United States, the Industrial Workers of the World was established in 1905 to radicalize the labor movement and engage in confrontations, sometimes violent, with management. The membership approached 100,000.

The Socialist Party, U.S. was formed in 1901 and grew to a membership of 118,000 in 1912 when it elected 56 Socialist mayors and tallied 900,000 votes for their presidential candidate. The Communist

1 Douglas Sloan, The Teaching of Ethics in the American Curriculum, 1876-1976, The Hastings Center Report, Hastings-on-Hudson NY, December 1979, pp. 21-23.

Party, U.S. was activated in 1919. In 1929, under the leadership of William Z. Foster, it became the leading revolutionary party in the United States.

Typically, college and university faculties attract a number of dissidents, who perceive colleges as primary agencies for social change. The powerful sway of socialist faculty members in American colleges was noted by Dr. Gordon Chalmers in his 1952 book, The Republic and the Person.

> The illusions of the Thirties had produced a timidity and lack of conviction among many Americans concerning the true nature of Nazism and its threat to democracy. One may add that they also produced a romanticized notion of the true nature of the communists. This sentimentalism was directly traceable to the ethical ignorance of persons thought to be learned. [Emphasis added] Many of these later admitted that the university world had persuaded the young that evil, itself, extensive and malignant, does not exist; that various explanations and terminologies can lead us to utopias both public and private; that statistics and organizations will set up alabaster cities "undimmed by human tears."[2]

No statement could more chillingly depict the insidious influence of socialists and revolutionaries in the second quarter of the 20th Century. On the campuses, the socialist ferment spread rapidly and intensely as more and more radicals were hired as professors.

RADICAL PROFESSORS

CARL ROGERS

In the 1960's, many Marxist and other anti-traditional and anti-American professors were powerful voices in the academic world. Carl Rogers was

2 Gordon Keith Chalmers, The Republic and the Person, Henry Regnery and Company, Chicago, 1952, p. 4.

one of the most influential psychologists in the country. He taught at Ohio State, Columbia University and the University of Chicago. He was the president of three national associations of psychologists and psychiatrists, and he received a number of distinguished awards. The following are excerpts from a Commencement Address he delivered at Sonoma State College in 1969. It was entitled, "The New Man."

> I see a New Man emerging . . . the person of tomorrow. I want to talk about him . . . I see him in campus unrest all over the world . . . in the racial unrest which runs like a fever through all our cities . . . He contradicts in his person almost every element of traditional schools, colleges, universities.
>
> Religious institutions are perceived as definitely irrelevant, and frequently damaging to human progress . . . He has distrust of marriage as an institution and little regard for vows of permanence . . .
>
> Currently he likes to be "turned on" by many kinds of experiences and by drugs . . . He often decides to obey those laws which he regards as just and to disobey those which he regards as unjust . . . He is active—sometimes violently, intolerantly and self-righteously, active in causes in which he believes.

The President of Sonoma State was so pleased with the speech, that he had it published and sent to college presidents throughout the country.

BILL AYERS

Bill Ayers was another revolutionary leader. As a student at the University of Michigan he joined and became an officer of SDS (Students for a Democratic Society). Ayers was influential in founding the Weatherman, an offshoot of SDS when it split up. The Weatherman was established to engage in violence and bombing. Three members of Weatherman were killed in a Greenwich Village townhouse explosion while trying to make bombs to set off at a party for soldiers at Fort Dix, New Jersey. After his participation in the Days of Rage riot in Chicago in

October of 1969, Ayers attended a "War Council" meeting in Michigan. One decision was to create an age of violence with bombs and armed robberies. Another decision was to establish underground groups in cities across the country. Ayers took part in bombings of the New York City Police Department Headquarters in 1970 and the United States Capitol Building in 1971.

The founding document of the Weatherman stated, "We are . . . a fighting force to achieve the destruction of U.S. imperialism and the achievement of a classless world: World Communism." A later document advocated a radical reformulation of sexual relations under the slogan "Smash Monogomy."

In an interview for the New York Times, Ayers said, "I don't regret setting the bombs. I feel we didn't do enough."[3]

On September 28, 2010, the Chicago Tribune reported that Bill Ayers, who had been a professor of education at the University of Illinois at Chicago for twenty-three years, had applied for Professor Emeritus status at the University, having retired recently. The request was unanimously rejected after the Board Chairman, Robert Kennedy's son, Christopher, said he could not grant the request of a man who dedicated one of his books to several people, including Sirhan Sirhan who assassinated his father.

H. BRUCE FRANKLIN

H. Bruce Franklin was another dynamic radical professor. In 1972, he was fired from a tenured position at Stanford for fomenting anti-war violence on campus. In a press interview, he said he hoped his dismissal would cause violence on campus . . . "This is a very violent place. There has to be counter-revolutionary violence." Franklin was subsequently appointed as a Distinguished Professor of English at Rutgers University serving many years.

In January of 1969, The American Enterprise Institute for Public Policy Research presented to an invited audience a debate about "Who Should Run The University" on three consecutive Thursday evenings. H. Bruce Franklin and I were the participants. I presented my paper the

3 Most of the material about Bill Ayers is drawn from a 9/24/10 Wikipedia commentary.

first Thursday and responded to questions. Franklin did the same on the second Thursday, and on the third, after receiving copies of each other's commentary, we responded to them before the final question period.

Here are several quotations from Franklin's initial speech.

> The multiuniversity is the wellspring of articulate bourgeois liberalism and the seedbed of the most outspoken radicalism . . . Who now actually does run the universities? . . . the answer is very simple: the owning class runs the universities, much as they run the rest of society . . .
>
> Anyone familiar with the American liberal left in the 1960s must realize that the faculty—and most faculties are now liberal, as they were in Russia 60 years ago, is overwhelmingly liberal . . .
>
> All power at Stanford legally derives from Leland Stanford's plunder through Mrs. Stanford's will . . .
>
> The sons and daughters of some of the wealthiest capitalists drop out; some take to the streets in rebellious demonstrations, some as a way of life. Many identify with the lifestyle and consciousness of the most oppressed and take as their heroes Malcolm X, Huey Newton, Ho Chi Minh, Che Guevera, and Mao Tse Tung.
>
> Last month [December 1969], at the annual convention of the Modern Language Association, which consists of 28,000 college and university teachers of all modern languages and literature, a serious rebellion took place. It was a rebellion against the establishment, against tradition, against the prevailing ideas of what a professor should be and against American imperialism. We passed a number of resolutions, including one denouncing the U.S. war against the Vietnamese people as "illegal, immoral and imperialistic" and demanding the immediate withdrawal of American and puppet forces . . . .
>
> In the final analysis, there can only be one radical position: the overwhelming majority of the people, that is the working class, must run the universities.

After the third session I asked Bruce if we could visit. He said he would like that. I asked how he got involved in radical activism. He said that while a student at a prominent Eastern College, he had a dynamic and persuasive professor who was a Marxist, and who eventually became a friend and his mentor. He recognized Bruce as a very bright student with drive and leadership qualities and enlisted him as a Communist. He told Bruce it would be well to train himself to be a professor at an elite university where he would be dealing with many students of wealth and future influence. The surest way to obtain a major university post would be to prepare himself in two fields, a standard one and another less traveled. He chose English and Science Fiction. His professor said that first he should experience the life and attitudes of the down-trodden by becoming a longshoreman.

In 1955-6 he was a tugboat deckhand and mate at the Pennsylvania RR marine Department, Pier H, Jersey City, New Jersey. After serving as a navigator and Intelligence Officer in the United States Air Force, he earned his Ph.D. in English and American Literature, and was hired as an Assistant Professor of English at Stanford, where he served for seven years. After a year at Johns Hopkins, he returned to Stanford and received many distinguished teaching awards. From 1975 to 1987 he was a Distinguished Professor of English at Rutgers University.

HERBERT MARCUSE

Herbert Marcuse, born in Germany, emigrated to the United States in 1934 and became a citizen. He served in the Office of War Information and then in the Office of Strategic Services (OSS). He taught at Harvard, Columbia and Brandeis from 1958 to 1965 and finally at the University of California at San Diego. He was a philosopher, sociologist and political theorist, and major analyst and advocate of Marxism. He was an anticapitalist and his writings strongly influenced many of the radical student activists including Angela Davis, Abbie Hoffman and the German revolutionary, Rudi Dutschke. His theories reenforced student radicalism and he was a frequent speaker at student protest gatherings. He was called "The Father of the New Left."

His concept of how to destroy American capitalism is credited with enormous influence in the success of the protest movement in doing away with the standards and ideals and restraints of America's free society. The large goal he had in mind was to alienate the youth from their families and adults, and undercut their patriotism. The first step was to persuade the young that Vietnam was an unjust war and urge them to defy the military draft which would drive their parents up the wall. The transition of the Free Speech movement to the Filthy Speech Movement served the same purpose, as did the slovenly dress. The Black Panthers, the Young Socialist Alliance and other organizations promoted the use of marijuana, which rapidly spread from campus to campus and was widely tolerated by university administrators.

The failure of the academic community to uphold the laws against the use of mind-altering drugs opened the door for the giant 1969 national festival of sex, drugs and rock music in Woodstock, New York. This was not just a mass offensive against morality and decency; it was, in fact, an insurrection, an open defiance of public law. In my judgment, the failure of the Federal Government to enforce public law and close down that festival made it inevitable that drug use thereafter would be uncontrollable. The civil order was trampled to death at Woodstock. America's fundamental respect for the laws was grievously reduced. Not long afterwards, people at Chicago's Lyric Opera were openly smoking marijuana in the foyer during the intermission.

Another goal promoted by Marcuse was to render ineffective the free society's rational method of resolving conflict which brings together representatives of opposing sides of an issue in order to arrive at an acceptable compromise. Under the new Marxist technique, the radical debater would assert some flat and flabbergasting lies and repeatedly insist upon them. The opponent, caught off guard, couldn't deal with even one of them.[4] The national radical campus organizations would insist that universities hold debates and would charge a rejection of academic freedom if they were turned down. Unfortunately, increasingly the political debates of our times often use the Marxist system of asserting lies. Another element of Marxist debates calls for the speaker to plant his flag far, far to the left of the current extreme leftist position and insist upon the validity of what he argues. Professor Eugene Genovese was the first major figure to assert he hoped the Vietnamese win

---

4 Information about Marcuse is drawn from http://en.Wikipedia.org/wiki/Herbert_Marcuse, www.uta.edu/huma/illuminations/kell12.htm and numerous conversations with radical students and student government officers at various colleges.

the war. This cry was repeated on campus after campus and the old leftermost position of immediate withdrawal of all troops soon became the moderate position.

The student protest movement also strongly advocated sexual liberation. Up until World War II all of America's coeducational colleges and universities had what were called parietal rules which required men students visiting in women's dormitories, and women in the men's dormitories to leave by a certain hour. All the majesty of American higher education, by policy, supported the standards of sexual behavior required for marriage and the family to be sustained as basic social institutions.

The first large eruption of student protest took place in December of 1964, at the University of California at Berkeley. It is said that the student activists were coached in their assertion that since the students were old enough to be drafted and killed in the Vietnam war, they were certainly old enough to decide how they lead their lives, so the parietal rules must be cancelled. The University agreed and the parietal rules were withdrawn. Many other colleges and universities across the country followed suit.

CHARLES HURST, JR. AND MICHAEL KLONSKY

On April 16, 1969, the John Madigan's "At Random" show on WBBM-TV in Chicago presented a program to discuss student unrest. The participants were Mike Klonsky, National Secretary of SDS (Students for a Democratic Society), Acting President of San Francisco State College S.I. Hayakawa, who was presiding over the "most tumultuous time" in The College's history," David Friedman, son of Milton Friedman, Charles Hurst, Jr., president of Crane Junior College, its first black president. He had closed the college on February 20 to commemorate the 4th anniversary of the slaying of Malcolm X, Dr. Rolf Weill, President of Roosevelt University in downtown Chicago. He had clashed with student groups and his office had been occupied by dissident factions. As President of Rockford College, I too, participated.

The program began as a discussion, but disintegrated into a shambles. President Hurst had said "Americans must accept radical change as the price of the nation's survival." President Hurst had chided President Hayakawa for his harsh suppression of student dissidents.

During a program break, President Weill asked President Hurst what he would do if angry students occupied his office. Hurst said that could never happen on his campus because everyone knew he would call in the Black Panthers and their resolution of the problem would not be very peaceful. When the break was over and we were back with an audience, David Friedman said to the TV audience that they should know what happened while they were gone and he told them. This infuriated President Hurst and Mike Klonsky came to his support. Hayakawa said to Klonsky he was backing a racist action. At that point a number of SDS members in the televising studio began to shout, "He called our boy a racist! He called our boy a racist! He called our boy a racist!" The rational discussion of "The Student Protest Movement" broke down, but the theatrics carried a message.

ANGELA DAVIS

Dartmouth's Professor Jeffrey Hart wrote an article[5] about black revolutionary Angela Davis who had given the keynote address for Dartmouth's celebration of fifteen years of co-education. She lectures frequently on campuses. She had just been appointed to the Presidential Chair at the University of California at Santa Cruz. She had studied philosophy with Herbert Marcuse, but had no academic credentials other than extensive involvement in 1960's protests.

Hart reports she had supplied guns for horrible crimes. In one of them, a Jonathan Jackson had tried to free from jail his convict brother. Jackson "went into a courthouse, took the judge prisoner and blew off his head with a shotgun. Angela Davis' name was on the gun's ownership papers. Twice Gus Hall ran for President on the Communist Party Ticket and chose Angela Davis as his Vice Presidential candidate. She won the Lenin Peace Prize from East Germany. And she was one of the most frequent campus speakers for the revolutionaries.

---

5 Jeffrey Hart, "Angela Davis, Academic Fraud," The Conservative Chronicle, 4/26/95.

MORE RADICAL ACTIVISM

A major listing of radical and revolutionary professors was published in a Special 1969 Edition of U.S.A. Magazine entitled, "The Detonators." Alice Widener, who founded the U.S.A. Publishing Company, had attended the Annual Conferences of Socialist Scholars during 1965, 66, 67, 68 and 69. They took place at Columbia University. Chancellor Maurice Mitchell of The University of Denver wrote an introduction for the published report of the meetings. "Alice Widener emerges as the only on-the-scene reporter of the underground planning that produced the campus violence in America and laid the foundations for a domestic revolution. These reports on the Socialist Scholars conferences are blunt, factual and significant notes of a great journalist. They are must reading for the survivors of the future." Barron's reprinted a condensed version of them.

The Chairman of the first panel was Professor H.H. Wilson of Princeton. Richard Hamilton, a Princeton Professor of Sociology, presented a paper on Working Class Authoritarianism. The word "authoritarian" during these sessions meant "anti-Communist, anti-Marxist, anti-radical-Socialist." The word "tolerant" meant sympathetic to radicalism, Marxism, socialism or Communism. Professor Hamilton identified the most intolerant elements of the population as farmers, self-employed middle class and factory foremen. Newspapers also were intolerant and so were veterans organizations.

During the week other speakers and panelists were from Brooklyn's Polytechnic Institute, Columbia, New York University, the radical Leftist Review, Bennington College, State University of New York at Plattsburg, California State College at Los Angeles, Pennsylvania State University, Amherst, Rutgers, Rhode Island College, Sarah Lawrence and Yale.

Sylvester Leaks of the Harlem Writers Guild who was preparing a biography of Malcolm X, spoke toward the end. These are quotations. "I am not non-violent. My leader was assassinated. I believe slavery and racism are the sine qua non of American society. The black lumpenproletariat should go to war now. The slogan they need is 'Burn, Baby, Burn." I believe we got to tear the system down now. We've got to stop the murderous, barbarous, American-imposed war in Vietnam. What is needed is a complete dismantling of the old morality."[6]

The Underground Press

Another exceedingly influential element of the student protest movement was the Alternative Media, or Underground Press. Many of the publications were staffed by radical students. All the underground media had a common commitment to the radical alteration or elimination of the traditional American institutions.

They pioneered the assault on the dominant taboos and traditions of the land. They were the training ground for the editors of the swiftly proliferating anti-American periodicals, as were the tracts published in the hippie communes. As the countercultural organizations multiplied, so did their publications that were sold or distributed on college and high school campuses and often military bases. For many of them, whatever their primary focus, the advocacy of marijuana use was a common theme. The number of these publications rose from a mere handful in 1964 to more than 400 in 1969 and more than 800 in 40 states in 1971. Increasingly, they identified with Che Guevara, Castro, Mao Tse Tung, Lenin, and Trostsky. Many of them moved deeper and deeper into the politics of the Far Left, justifying this transition by claiming "complete frustration in trying to work within the system." These papers supported and reinforced the protest movements by encouraging defiance of the draft, and the use of illegal drugs, gutter language, praising the joys of sexual promiscuity, and self-righteously asserting the right to do these things.

The Institute of Policy Studies, instigated by the SDS, sponsored two periodicals. One of them, Mother Jones, claimed a paid circulation of 275,000 in three years. It was named for an indefatigable labor movement organizer. She helped establish The Industrial Workers of the World. She was a prominent advocate of the Mexican Revolution. Once when she was introduced to a college audience as "a great humanitarian," she interrupted to shout, "No! I'm a hell-raiser." The magazine named for her dwelt on activities of "The Left." Typical subjects were favorable articles

---

6 Alice Widener, The Detonators, USA Publishing Company, New York City, pp. 4-7, 1969.

about the Castro Regime in Cuba, Palestinian gorillas, Communist elements in the Portuguese Turmoil and VietCong.

Take Over was a periodical published in Madison, Wisconsin. In one issue it presented a plan for financing the revolution. It listed the names, companies and home addresses of forty top executives of major corporations and the amount that each company could afford to pay as ransom when they were kidnapped. That amount was determined according to the formula used in corporate kidnappings in South America. The article presented a technique that might be used in kidnapping Ray Kroc, the founder of McDonald's. On his daily ride to the office, he is driven through a narrow alley. Wagons filled with pumpkins could be tipped over at the ends of the alley, making him a captive.

The Underground Press, virtually unknown to the public, exerted a wide and powerful influence on the youth of the 1960s and 1970s.[7]

---

7 Material about The Underground Press is drawn from The Alternative Media, written by Frank Watson, Jr., who had served in the Military Intelligence. The book was published by the The Rockford College Institute, Rockford, IL in 1979.

FEDERAL FUNDS FOR COLLEGES: BLESSING OR CALAMITY?

Until well into the twentieth century, academic leaders were held in high regard by the public. Indeed, some university presidents achieved the status of senior statesmen in the society. One of them was Dr. Nicholas Murray Butler who headed Columbia University for forty-three years. Earlier he had founded and was president of the New York College for the Training of Teachers, later renamed Teachers College. He also was President of the Carnegie Foundation for International Peace and shared the 1931 Nobel Peace Prize with Jane Addams.

Dr. Butler's 1921 Annual Report to the Trustees of Columbia University dwelt at length on the question of federal aid to education. What follow are excerpts from that report:

> One of the most noteworthy of recent developments in American life is the zeal with which machinery is designed and built ostensibly to serve various public interests and undertakings, but in reality to control them. Perhaps in no other way is the decline of faith in liberty so clearly marked . . . When anything appears to go wrong, or when any desirable movement seems to lag, a cry goes up for the creation of some new board or commission, and for the appropriation of public funds to maintain it in reasonable comfort. An infinite number of blank forms must be filled and an infinite number of records must be kept, classified and audited at steadily mounting cost . . .
>
> So far as education is concerned, there has been over-organization for a long time past. Too many persons are

> engaged in supervising, in inspecting and in recording the work of other persons. There is too much machinery and in consequence, a steady temptation to lay more stress upon the form of education than upon its content. [Emphasis added] Statistics displace scholarship. There are, in addition too many precise laws and not enough opportunity for those mistakes and failures, due to individual initiative and experiment, which are the foundation for great and lasting success.
>
> It is now proposed to bureaucratize and to bring into uniformity the educational system of the whole United States, while making the most solemn assurance that nothing of the kind is intended. The glory and the successes of education in the United States are due to its freedom, to its uniqueness, to its reflection of the needs and ambitions and capacities of local communities, and to its being kept in close and constant touch with the people themselves. There is not enough money in the United States, even if every dollar of it were expended on education, to produce by federal authority, or what is naively called cooperation between the Federal Government and the several states, educational results that would be at all comparable with those that have already been reached under the free and natural system that has grown up among us . . . [8]

The strident agitation for Federal Aid continued in the next two decades. A formal rebuttal was mounted in 1945. The Problems and Policies Committee of the American Council on Education and the Educational Policies Committee of the National Educational Association met in emergency joint session. According to President Millikan of the California Institute of Technology, the participants in this meeting were twenty of the most distinguished educators in the United States. They issued "A Statement of Alarm" to the citizens of the United States. It began:

---

8 From the personal papers of Dr. Cowling, president emeritus of Carleton College, now stored at the Howard Center on Family, Religion and Society, Rockford, Illinois.

> For more than a quarter of a century and especially during the last decade, education in the United States, like a ship caught in a powerful tide, has drifted ever farther into the dangerous waters of federal control and domination.
>
> The drift has continued at an accelerating rate during the war. Present signs indicate that unless it is sharply checked by an alert citizenry, it will continue even more rapidly after the war . . .
>
> It is the deliberate and reasoned judgment of the two educational commissions who join in the appeal which this document makes to the people of the United States that the trend toward the federalizing of education is one of the most dangerous on the current scene . . .
>
> While it is recognized that new factors in contemporary civilization require closer organization and increased centralization of some areas of life, other areas can be permitted to come under central control only at our peril . . . Education should be placed high on the list of services to be continued under state and local control.[9]

The National Education Association's Educational Policies Committee that joined in writing and publicizing this document clearly did not represent the members and the paid staff of the National Education Association. That Association, the NEA, became an advocate for Federal funding. The following material is quoted from a pamphlet it published entitled, "The Root of Opposition to Federal Aid to Education."

> The fight over federal aid to education is, on the surface, a political fight with spicy dashes of racial prejudice and religious bitterness thrown in. But under the surface, in reality, it is an economic battle—one of the oldest and hardest fought in this country. It falls in the classic

9 Robert A. Millikan, Statement issued at the California Institute of Technology, June 7, 1949, pp. 2, 3. (Now with the Cowling papers at the Howard Center.)

> pattern of historic battles between the haves and the have-nots, between those who control the wealth of the land and those who make up the masses . . .
>
> The truth of the matter is that the minority, who are the elite financially and culturally, do not trust democracy very far . . .
>
> On the other hand, the majority, while it admits to something patriotic in the word 'capitalism,' particularly since it has become an antonym of 'communism,' nevertheless exerts most of its political energy—and has been doing so since the last century—controlling, curtailing and transforming capitalism to some forms and stages of socialism . . .

So the fight has developed and grown . . . a fight between the people with the wealth, and the people with the kids.[10]

Also typical of the heated argumentation was this July 18, 1948 editorial from the New Haven Register.

> President Truman has elected to include the socialistic $300,000,000 Federal aid to education program among the items he offers for the consideration of the July 25 special session of Congress. This, stripped of its wordy camouflage, has nothing whatsoever to offer to the cause of the equality of educational opportunity or the logical advancement of education and education facilities. It does not represent a sincere or worthy program for consideration at this time, or any time.
>
> It was not accident that caused Mr. Truman to inject his proposal into the political stream at this time. It was done deliberately and with a set purpose. First and foremost, it is expressive of the centralized, planned economy, reckless spending philosophy upon which this Administration and its predecessors have been based.

---

10 Pamphlet published and distributed by The Division of Federal Relations, National Education Association, 1201 16th Street, NW, Washington, DC. Copy in the files of The Howard Center, 934 N. Main Street, Rockford, IL 61103.

Beyond this it has been injected at this time because of its class and group prejudice-raising potentials.

That it would be raised as an issue of the campaign was a foregone conclusion. A preview of this fact was to be found in the recent Massachusetts sessions of the Harvard Summer School Conference on Educational Administration. There one Howard A. Dawson, director of Rural Services for the National Educational Association, chose to charge House Speaker Martin and Majority Leader Halleck with "dictatorial tactics" in opposing and blocking Federal aid to education in the 80th Congress.[11]

THE FLOODGATES OF ENORMOUS AMOUNTS OF MONEY FOR CAMPUSES BLASTED OPEN

The impassioned contention about federal aid was brought to an abrupt halt on October 4, 1957. On that day the Soviet Union launched Sputnik, its world-circling satellite. The Soviet Union had leap-frogged America's technological advantage. It was a staggering breakthrough with ominous military repercussions. On September 2, 1958, the U.S. Congress passed the National Defense Education Act.

Section 101 of Title I states: The Congress hereby finds and declares that the security of the Nation requires the fullest development of the mental resources and technical skills of its young men and women. The present emergency demands that additional and more adequate educational opportunities be made available . . . It is therefore the purpose of this Act to provide substantial assistance in various forms to individuals and to states in order to insure trained manpower sufficient to meet the national defense needs of the United States.

Section 102 is titled "Federal Control of Education is Prohibited." It asserts "Nothing contained in this Act shall be construed to authorize any department, agency, officer or employee of the United States to exercise any direction, supervision or control over the curriculum, program of instruction, administration, or personnel of any education or school system."

---

[11] This editorial is in the Cowling papers at The Howard Center.

Among other things, the Act authorized loans for students and for the construction of educational facilities, and financial assistance for strengthening science, mathematics and modern foreign language instruction.

From the beginning, the solemn and comprehensive prohibition of any involvement of governmental personnel in the conduct of an educational program was largely disregarded. In 1963, a group of college presidents—I was among them—visited a number of members of Congress and officials from the Office of Education with a proposal to substitute tax credits for gifts to colleges in place of Federal grants. When we explained the plan to Dr. Francis Keppel, the U.S. Commissioner of Education, he said "We couldn't allow that! It would prevent us from accomplishing our social objectives!" It was his intention to convert the educational institutions into agencies for achieving social objectives determined by the Federal government. Commissioner Keppel had just proven that the worst fears of what would happen to education if it were Federalized, had already been fulfilled.

For generations, Americans have been wary of any intrusion by the church into governmental affairs. The separation of education and state is every bit as important as the church/state separation. Most Americans have only a meager understanding of what a free society is. It is generally taken for granted, like electricity, and only becomes a matter of concern if it is taken away. The magnitude of the threat to America's liberty by the governmental usurpation of the primary responsibility for the nation's schooling is so great that a review of the nature and the blessings of liberty is essential. What follows is the text of a speech I gave in 2007.

LIBERTY REVISITED

By John A. Howard, presented April 26, 2007
to the Rotary Club of Rockford, Illinois

Liberty Revisited. A little story will be a helpful lead-in to this theme. It's about a medieval knight. Late one afternoon, he was returning to the castle, and he was a pitiful sight to see. His horse was limping and he was skewgee in the saddle. His armor was dented, his lance was broken and the proud plume on his helmet was crumpled and hung down over his face. The Lord of the castle saw him coming and rushed out to meet him. "What terrible thing has befallen you, Sir Percy?" he asked.

"Oh, sire," he said, "I have been laboring all day in your service, robbing and pillaging your enemies to the West.

"You've been doing what!!" exclaimed the nobleman.

Thinking he was hard of hearing, the knight replied, much louder, "I have been robbing and pillaging your enemies to the West."

"But I haven't any enemies to the West," was the horrified reply.

"Oh!" said the knight. And then, "Well, I think you do now."

There is a moral to this story. Enthusiasm is not enough. You have to have a sense of direction.

For a long time, Meg Greenfield wrote the editorials on the last page of Newsweek. On December 14, 1998, when she knew she didn't have long to live, she wrote a chilling wake-up call to America. It seems to have disappeared down the memory hole without causing even a sigh from the dormant conscience of the readers.

Her opening statement was

> You look around political Washington for a public figure in an important position of power who also has moral authority, and you will find none. Those in the leadership of both parties who have not been dirtied up in their own political scandals have leapt eagerly to the defense of those on their side who have, shamelessly justifying every kind of sleaziness committed by their party on the ground that the other side does it, too . . . or that the campaign needed the money . . . or that the other side over-reacted . . . or something."

The situation she describes is, itself, cause for dismay, but the shattered principle it reflects foretells grave and lasting troubles for us. We need to know that morality is the essential and irreplaceable foundation of a free society. For several generations Americans have not known how precious freedom is to the human soul. The harrowing tales of the Cubans risking, and sometimes losing, their lives as they tried to reach freedom in the United States, and the comparable reports of East Germans gunned down as they tried to scale the Berlin Wall and of innumerable boat people drowned or captured as they fled from Communism in Southeast Asia—all these were for us just tragic stories in the news, seemingly unrelated to life in America. The absolute and ultimate importance of liberty to all those refugees simply didn't register with us. FREEDOM WAS MORE IMPORTANT THAN LIFE TO ALL OF THEM.

Furthermore, Americans haven't a clue as to what liberty is, or how to sustain it. The British statesman Edmund Burke was a wise and eminent political philosopher and an ardent and articulate champion of liberty. He stated that extreme liberty, which would seem to be perfect liberty, is instead, its fatal flaw. Perfect liberty doesn't exist anywhere and shouldn't exist anywhere because, he said, "liberty must be limited to be possessed."

It is startling for us that he should speak of a fault of liberty, for liberty in our minds is a pure unencumbered blessing with no room for anyone to say, "Yes, but." It jars us to be told that there must be limitations. Actually, the limitations he had in mind were not primarily legal restrictions.

> Manners are more important than laws. Upon them, in a great measure, the laws depend. Manners are what vex or soothe, corrupt or purify, exalt or debase, barbarize or refine us . . . According to their quality, they aid morals . . . or they totally destroy them.

Burke's declaration that political liberty cannot exist unless it is sustained by moral behavior was a truth thoroughly known to and embraced by our Founding Fathers.

President John Adams' Second Inaugural Address was the first one given in the new Capitol Building. He urged: "May this be the residence of virtue and happiness. Here and throughout our country, may simple manners, pure morals, and true religion flourish forever."[12]

President James Madison wrote, "We have staked the whole future of American civilization, not upon the power of government, far from it. We have staked the

---

12 John Adams, Gleaves Whitney, American Presidents: Farewell Messages to the Nation, Landham MD, Lexington Books, 2003, p. 32.

future of all our political institutions upon the capacity of mankind for self-government; upon the capacity of each and all of us to govern ourselves according to the Ten Commandments of God.[13]

President John Quincy Adams wrote, "The highest glory of the American Revolution was this: It connected in one indissoluble bond the principles of civil government with the principles of Christianity."[14]

The solemn, religious character of these quotations reminds us that the first New England colonists uprooted their families to brave the perilous ocean voyage and the appalling dangers and difficulties of establishing a settlement in the wilderness for one purpose only—to attain freedom, a special kind of freedom, religious freedom. To be free to practice their religion was their only objective. That was the beginning of a new civilization of Christendom. That term does not imply that everyone was a Christian. Rather it denotes an area where the people, whatever their beliefs about God, live according to the tenets of Christianity. It was 170 years after the Plymouth Colony was established, that the American nation was founded as a political entity of Christendom.

The French historian Alexis de Tocqueville visited America in the 1830's. His book Democracy in America is a classic description of the government and of the life of the people in America. Here are a few excerpts.

> Christianity directs domestic life. Of all the countries in the world, America is the one in which the marriage tie is the most respected and where the highest and truest conception of conjugal happiness

13 William J. Federer, Treasury of Presidential Quotations, St. Louis, Mo., AmeriSearch, 2002, p. 34.

14 David Barton, The Myth of Separation, Wallbuilders Press, 1991, Aledo TX, p. 86. MacDowell and Beliles, America's Providential History, pp. 263-4.

has been conceived . . . Christianity reigns without obstacles by universal consent . . . [15]

In another chapter he writes,

In the United States, the Motherland's presence is everywhere. It is a subject of concern to the village and to the whole union. The inhabitants care for each of the country's interests as if it were their own.[16]

And later –

By their practice, Americans show they feel the urgent necessity to instill morality into democracy by means of religion. What they think of themselves in this respect enshrines a truth which should penetrate deep into the consciousness of every democratic nation.[17]

Instill morality into democracy by means of religion—De Tocqueville saw this as the only means by which liberty can be perpetuated in all democratic nations.

In the First World War, every doughboy going overseas received from the government a New Testament for his knapsack. Christendom still prevailed.

Fast forward now to 1939. That was the year of the New York World's Fair. In the early 1930's the Great Depression had been a disaster so severe it is today unimaginable. Millions of people had no job and millions lost their homes to mortgage foreclosure. Still the Christian decency of Americans remained solid. Rates of robbery and theft did not skyrocket. People did what they could to help relatives and neighbors. The real America of pre-World War II was captured

---

15 Alexis De Tocqueville, Democracy in America, Doubleday and Company, Garden City, New York, NY, 1969, p. 78.

16 De Tocqueville, op. cit. p. 98.

17 De Tocqueville, op. cit. p. 77.

in a book entitled 1939, The Lost World of the Fair by David Galernter. It offers a portrait of the people, their character and their sentiments. Here are a few glimpses.

> New York's Mayor LaGuardia was a legendary, honest servant of the people. "And by the way," a guidebook cautioned, "Don't try any funny stuff. New York was the best policed city of the world." . . .
>
> At popular Jones Beach State Park on Long Island, the flag was lowered by a uniformed staff to the strains of the National Anthem every evening while every bather, picnicker, stroller, game player and onlooker stood at attention . . .
>
> In 1939, men wore suits or occasionally sport jackets to a fair. Women wore dresses or sometimes a blouse and skirt. Most adults wore a hat.
>
> An American of this era freely accepts certain obligations . . . He lives by the rules because they are the rules, because they give a community a shape, coherence and a shared viewpoint. Thirties America is a rules-following society, an "ought" culture.[18]

At the time of Pearl Harbor, the standards of Christendom were still generally observed, but as David Galernter implied, that condition resulted more from the momentum of long established custom than from the dominance of religion in daily American life.

Manners and morals do not come naturally to a human being. The acculturation of the young for life in Christendom is carried on by religion, by the families, by educational institutions, by literature and other cultural influences. And the support of these codes of conduct had to be continually reenforced by the culture. Here is one small example of that reenforcement at work.

---

[18] David Galernter, The Lost World of the Fair, Avon Bouhs, New York NY, 1995, p. 163.

When our son was baptized in 1956, the clergyman, a much loved pastor nearing the end of his career, asked the family members to gather around the altar. The minister, having received the baby from my wife, said slowly and quietly, "What I hold in my arms, good friends, is God's greatest gift, a new life. This child at this time is a wonder of potential. How that potential may develop, for better or worse, will mainly be determined by the people gathered at this altar, his family. I charge you to remember that the shaping of this life is in your hands, and I pray that with God's help you may encourage and cultivate that which is good and kind and wholesome, and I pray that you will discover and shield him from that which is self-centered, corrupt and cruel." Such ceremonies were reminders to all in attendance of their on-going responsibilities to their children.

The role of literature in nurturing the character of the people was brought into focus half a century ago when the Saturday Review of Literature published an editorial denouncing an award bestowed by The Library of Congress on Ezra Pound for a book of poetry.

> While one must divorce politics from art, it is quite another matter to use the word "politics" as a substitute for values. We do not believe that art has nothing to do with values . . . We do not believe that a poet can shatter ethics and still be a good poet. We do not believe that poetry can convert words into maggots that eat at human dignity and still be good poetry.[19]

The problem is certainly not how to prevent an Ezra Pound, or anyone else, from writing whatever seems important to him. The magazine's editors were concerned with what the community shall prize and praise. What shall be the values and ideals which shape

---

19 Editorial, The Saturday Review of Literature, July 2, 1949.

the life of the society, and how can those ideals be perpetuated. The editors were insisting that those who hold major responsibilities in the realm of public beliefs are inexcusably delinquent if they contribute to the destruction of standards of civilized conduct. An echo of Edmund Burke, a century and a half later.

There were many causes contributing to the collapse of our "ought" society. Of course, the most powerful one of all, and the one which in recent years has extensively eroded the public commitment to all standards of morality has been the ever-growing, relentless attack on the Christian religion. The morals and manners of piety, truthfulness, honesty, generosity, faithfulness, kindness, helpfulness, integrity and conscientious civic duty were aspects of the way of life of the Christians who settled America. Christendom wasn't introduced to them in the New World. It simply described the civilization they brought with them. Until the second half of the Twentieth Century, the individuals and organized groups, wishing to do away with one or more of the settled standards of behavior had an uphill battle because they were challenging conduct prescribed by the Bible.

Solzhenitsyn, in his Templeton Prize speech, provides the Communist example of revolutionaries' inevitable assault on religion.

> It was Dostoyevski who drew from the French Revolution and its seething hatred of the Church the lesson that "revolution must necessarily begin with atheism. That is absolutely true . . . Within the philosophical system of Marx and Lenin, and at the heart of their psychology, hatred of God is the principal driving force, more fundamental than all their political and economic pretensions."[20]

---

[20] Alexander Solzhenitsyn, National Review, July 22, 1983.

This is not a surprising feature of revolution for if people have a fixed and cherished allegiance to God, the perpetrators of the new order must destroy or, at least demean and smother that allegiance. They cannot tolerate an authority superior to their own. In America, the cultural revolution being waged by moral anarchists has been gathering steam for four decades, contaminating our social institutions and eating away at the general observance of many standards of Christendom.

A few illustrations of compromised institutions:

> Testimony before the Nixon Drug Commission by a university Chancellor revealed that his university's public literature notified students they would be subject to disciplinary action if they had in their possession more than one week's supply of marijuana. All the students of that university were officially informed that it's OK to break the law, if you do it in moderation.[21]
>
> On April 17, 2002, the United States Supreme Court handed down a decision stating which sort of child pornography was legal.
>
> On April 9, 2002, there was a full-page ad in the New York Times urging the legalization of marijuana. It featured a large picture of Michael Bloomberg, the Mayor of New York City, saying about smoking marijuana, "You bet I did and I enjoyed it." Proud and open defiance of the law from one in a position of exalted authority is devastating to civic order.

On July 5, 2002, the Wall Street Journal reported that a new poll by Zogby International found that three quarters of all college seniors believe that the difference between right and wrong is relative. What can one expect when members of the Do-Your-Own-Thing

---

21 I served on the National Commission on Marijuana and Drug Abuse and took notes on this testimony.

Generation control most of the levers of power and persuasion?

The cultural revolution has been spearheaded by pseudo-civilized agitators who believe human judgment should prevail over God's judgment, if there is a God. They acknowledge no supreme source of moral authority. They have effectively destroyed our free society's system of resolving conflict. Lacking the graces of truthfulness, open-mindedness and restraint—traits of character essential for peaceably adjudicating disputes—the moral anarchists have developed great skills in demonizing those who disagree with them, turning their opponents into objects of fear, hatred and scorn. False witness is their primary weapon in advancing their campaigns. What was once amicable America is now belligerent America.

What has the repression of Christian standards of behavior accomplished? Are children safer and happier? Is the emotional stability of adults in this era of the free-wheeling sexual life-style any greater? Do the citizens have a greater respect than before for the government, the schools, the press, the judiciary and other social institutions? Do the people trust one another more nowadays? Returning to Edmund Burke's analysis of the impact of manners, we ask if the manners of our time soothe and refine us? Or do they corrupt and barbarize us? Is America's performance on the manners scale what we truly want?

I was once interviewed on a National Public Radio Talk Show by a bright and articulate college student. I had mentioned that in a properly functioning free society, the people can go about their daily lives trusting each other and not worrying whether someone might harm or cheat them. The young host of the show asked, "Have we ever had a civilization like that?" He surprised me. He was perfectly serious.

I told him when I was a child in the late 1920's my younger brother and I would walk half a mile after dark

> through a park and across a railroad track to attend a program at the Community House. Our parents had no reason whatever to worry about us. Sometimes our family would drive into Chicago for a day. We parked the car unlocked, often with clothes or packages in it. Even when the keys were left in the ignition, the car and its contents would still be there.
>
> Now, it was the Talk Show host who was startled. He blurted out, "I can't even imagine such a time!" How low have we fallen if the young people, even the highly educated and intelligent ones, haven't a glimmer of understanding about the relatively crime-free, friendly, helpful, "ought" society that used to prevail in their own country?
>
> The absence of moral authority in government, so painfully lamented by Meg Greenfield now spreads across the whole spectrum of vocations. And liberty languishes.
>
> America has lost its sense of direction. Liberty was once the compass by which America steered its course. Not even knowing now what liberty is, Americans find that no direction is forward.

This speech endeavors to make it clear why a free society is so crucially dependent upon the character of the people, not just for its success but for its very survival. The triumph of the anti-American radicalism in trashing the traditions and doing away with the standards of civilized behavior has profoundly jeopardized America's once flourishing free society.

A broad segment of the vocabulary has become obsolete because the concepts which it embodied have been rejected. Modesty, decency, probity, rectitude, honor, politeness, virtue, magnanimity, chastity, piety, righteousness, propriety—these and many other terms of approved behavior have been consigned to limbo. They don't even enter into public discussion and decision-making. Naturally, their opposites have suffered the same fate: terms such as vile, licentious, malign, dissolute, roué, shame, disgrace, evil, sin, stigma, ostracize, iniquity, and so on. Any concerted effort to reestablish a civil order in America has been made far more difficult by the coarseness of campus life, tolerated, and in some places encouraged by campus policies.

The absence of moral authority lamented by Meg Greenfield referred to the self-centered alumni of the 1960s' colleges who had risen to powerful positions in Washington. New York University's Professor Michael Blonsky was an analyst of cultural trends. He was interviewed in 1992 by the Chicago Tribune at NIKE TOWN, a glittering new store on Michigan Avenue that sells wildly expensive sneakers. "This," said Blonsky, entering the store, "is a church! A post-modern church!" Then, pointing to a life-sized figure of basketball star Michael Jordan, he declared, "Look! There's God!" This was not just crude and blasphemous flippancy.

He went on to explain that many people today are totally unpersuaded by any system of beliefs. For them flashy shoes are as important as anything gets. Beyond a fascination with impressive things, Blonsky cited as other values of the New Culture: glamour, fitness, youth, power, freedom, eroticism and violence. "In the 1960s and 1970s," Blonsky noted, "the human psyche began to be recoded, it got altered. The feeling is people are being produced that are different from before World War II."[22]

In pondering the question of what good education is it may be helpful to consider the nature of the American society referred to by Professor Blonsky prior to World War II. Here is a speech I gave fifty years after the assault on Pearl Harbor.

---

[22] Paul Galloway, "Code-Buster, Michael Blonsky dissects the signs of our times." The Chicago Tribune, 9 September 1992, Sect. 2, Pages 1, 2.

WORLD WAR II, HALF A CENTURY AND A WHOLE CIVILIZATION AGO

By John A. Howard 15 December 1991
for the Rockford Rotary Club

Japan's assault on Pearl Harbor was a thunderbolt that exploded in every living room in the United States. The battles and the bombing and the destruction in Europe which Americans had been watching from the balcony for two years were instantly no longer just somber news reports, but a terrible, frightening reality that had taken command of our lives.

For the men of draft age, the ultimate question of human existence was starkly catapulted to the top of the agenda. Are we merely clever animals that some improbable quirk of evolution has delivered, or are we children of God placed here with obligations to Him and to other human beings? Does the individual seek to save his own skin as his first and over-riding concern? Or are there ideals and linkages and duties that compellingly call him to serve his country's flag?

At the time and over the months that followed, many Americans volunteered for military duty, and millions were drafted with all but a small handful of them responding readily and serving creditably in the capacities to which they were assigned.

I was a member of a tank battalion in the First Infantry Division. Our unit participated in the D-Day landings in Normandy. Eleven months later, we met the Russians in Czechoslovakia as the European part of the war came to an end. Most of the eleven months we were under enemy fire.

It is difficult for a person who hasn't experienced it to imagine what combat is like or to conceive of the emotional stress that accumulates. It is a shock to fire weapons at other human beings, and kill them; to adjust to a continuing series of deaths of people you have worked closely with and liked and counted on; to come to terms with the fear for your own life; to bear responsibility for life and death decisions some of which turn out badly for your comrades; to carry on through prolonged periods with next to no sleep; to spend day after day never knowing what will happen the next minute.

The point of all this is not to drum up sympathy and applause fifty years after the fact. Rather I want to focus on the performance of America's civilian military forces in that conflict. Despite relentless emotional stress, only a very small percentage of the troops in our battalion had psychological breakdowns, or combat fatigue as it was called, and not many turned to alcohol or drugs as an escape mechanism. The national psyche in that era was sturdy and resilient. And needed to be, not only for the pressures of fighting, but also for the ordeal of the training process.

Think for a minute about the raw material that became America's fighting troops. Our battalion was drafted from the state of Illinois. We had farm boys and factory workers, accountants and dish-washers, grocers and truck-drivers; we had a whole United Nations of Chicago ethnic groups; we had athletes and couch potatoes, we had people with graduate degrees and drop-outs. America's task was to forge them into a physically-fit, alert fighting force trained in the use of complex, weapons, battlefield tactics, and other realms of mortally important knowledge.

Not only were the civilian recruits a mixed bag, but so were the people who trained them. The teachers were regular army sergeants and corporals. In order to provide sufficient instructional staff for the avalanche of draftees, many army regulars were pressed into teaching service who would not have been in normal circumstances. Patience and helpfulness were not then standard concerns in the military training process. Techniques of encouragement for slow learners often consisted of shouting, cursing, humiliating, and punishing. It was an amazing feat of forbearance and learner determination for civilian America to rise above the heavy-handed indignities of the training process and somehow come to know the things that had to be known to fight a war.

What were the features and conditions of the American reality fifty years ago that prepared the general populace to accept military service, to be undaunted by and profit from a crude training system, and to remain on an even keel emotionally through the rigors of warfare? There are, of course, no simple answers, but there are, I believe, some elements of the culture which had a powerful impact in shaping the character of the people of that time.

One was set forth in the book, *Man's Search for Meaning*, a narrative about one of Adolph Hitler's death camps. The author, Victor Frankl, was an Austrian physician, incarcerated because he was a Jew. The prisoners were subjected to unbelievable extremes of cruelty, privation, and persecution. They had inadequate clothing and housing and almost no food. They were forced to live in filth and were given no medical care. Dr. Frankl did what little he could for the sick and dying. Over a period of time, his physician's habit of observing the health of the people around him led to an astonishing discovery. The people who kept their strength and sanity the longest were not the ones who by brute strength or clever tricks obtained more than their share of the scarce food, but rather those who tried to be helpful to the other prisoners and shared with them what little they had. Their physical and mental condition seemed to be strengthened by their friendliness, their compassion, and their primary attentions devoted to something other than themselves.

At first, Dr. Frankl found this hard to believe, but as the months went by, his observation was thoroughly confirmed. It was clear to him that no matter how wretched and hopeless a situation may be, the individual has the freedom to choose how he will respond to that situation, and if the response is one of trying to make life better for others, that effort reinforces the individual's psychological and physical stamina.[23]

Anyone who was old enough for military duty on December 7, 1941, had lived through the Great Depression. That phenomenon scarcely rates a footnote in today's history books, but it was, I assure you, a formative influence in the character of a generation of Americans. Consider, for example, the impact on the labor force. Jobs were scarce and people soon learned, if they didn't already know, that the employees who helped each other and did all they could to make the operation successful had the best chance of keeping their jobs. If the boss was a grouch or didn't seem very bright, the worker still needed to do his best to find ways to get along with his employer. The folks who were always thinking about themselves, the quarrelsome ones and the chronic complainers, soon discovered they were not needed.

The financial bind of the depression had an impact on children, too. If they could obtain part-time work delivering newspapers, or putting stock on the shelves of a store, or shining shoes, that income helped to put bread on the table. It also gave to the children an early experience in the satisfaction of being helpful, and a justifiable sense of self-worth. With little money available

---

23 Information about Viktor Frankl is drawn from his book, Man's Search for Meaning, Beacon Press
Boston, 2006.

for entertainment, and with no television, children read more than they do now. They played sandlot games of softball and touch football and learned how to get along with one another without the adult supervision of coaches and referees. The need to "make do" in the necessities of the household as well as in recreation was a good teacher of cooperation and independence.

Pre-World War II was also vastly different from today in the religious dimensions of American life. The importance of religion to emotional health was set forth by the Swiss psychiatrist Carl Jung. He wrote:

> Over the past thirty-five years, people from all the civilized countries of the earth have consulted me . . . . There has not been one whose problem has not been finding a religious outlook of life. It is safe to say that every one of them fell ill because he had lost that which the living religions of every age have given to their followers, and none of them has been really healed who did not regain his religious outlook.[24]

He was referring to the peace and stability that comes to the person who acknowledges a deity and a fixed set of ideals that provide a framework for living. America began as a religious nation and prior to World War II it was still widely assumed that people believed in God and belonged to a church or synagogue. The "'til death do us part" in the marriage vows was still regarded as a commitment to God. Divorce was infrequent and there was a stigma and an embarrassment that fell on those who did divorce. Blasphemy was not a subject for literature or for joking.

The respect for other people's religious commitments was such that no large private party or public event was held on Friday evening that did not provide a fish entrée

---

[24] Carl G. Jung, Modern Man in Search of a Soul, London, Kegan Paul, 1933, p. 244.

for the Roman Catholics in attendance, for in those days avoiding meat on that day was obligatory for them. The newspapers and magazines had no qualms about printing testimonies of religious faith. A particularly powerful one was printed as the editorial for *U.S. News and World Report* and was reprinted again several years later. It was written by Madame Chang Kai-shek in 1943 at the time she and her husband were trying to rally the Chinese people in territories already captured by the Communists. Here is an excerpt from her statement:

> Prayer is our source of guidance and balance. God is able to enlighten the understanding. I am often bewildered because my mind is only finite. I question and doubt my own judgments. Then I seek guidance and when I am sure, I go ahead, leaving the results with Him . . . I do not think it is possible to make this understandable to one who has not tried it. To explain to one who has no experience of getting guidance what it means would be like trying to make a stone-deaf person understand the beauty of a Chopin sonata.
>
> What I do want to make clear is that whether we get guidance or not, it is there. It is like tuning in on the radio. There's music in the air whether we tune in or not . . . With me religion is a very simple thing. It means to try with all my heart and soul and strength and mind to do the will of God.

It wasn't until 1947 that the United States Supreme Court suddenly discovered that the First Amendment to the Constitution contained language that implied a wall of separation between church and state, although no such language appears in the text. Before that time biblical stories and biblical quotations and religious literature and prayers were an important and wholly expected element of American education in the public schools and colleges as well as the private ones. The impact of the banishment of God and faith and prayer from the educational process was manifest in national surveys conducted by the Princeton Religious Research Center founded by George Gallup.

A poll conducted in 1952 revealed that 64% of the 18-24 age group, whose schooling had taken place for the most part prior to the Supreme Court Decision, stated that religion was very important in their lives. Twenty-six years later only 37% of the same age group considered religion important in their lives. In 1958, 40% of the under 30 age group attended church weekly. Nineteen years later that figure had dropped to 29%. There was a 40% drop in both categories after the Supreme Court cleansed the schools of religion. Obviously, America's troops in World War II were the beneficiaries of the earlier kind of schooling.

Another dimension of the America fifty years ago was the centrality of the family in the life of the people. We have already noted the children's role in helping to earn income in the depression and have indicated the infrequency of divorce. More needs to be said. Fourteen years ago our Rockford Institute sponsored the first national conference on the importance of the family and the need to reverse family disintegration. One of the speakers on that occasion talked about his own family and said that although they had very little money, they had everything money can't buy. I have never read an essay that describes more accurately than that small phrase the blessings which a family can provide to its children. Most Americans going into military service in the 1940's carried with them the benefits of having lived in an intact family.

I want to conclude this rather subjective reflection on what America seemed to be in the 1940's with a quotation from one letter, the full text of another and a final comment. The first is a passage from the letter my mother tucked into my pocket as I went out the door to report for military service.

None of us knows what is in store for us in this life, but one thing is certain: if we live according to the noblest ideals of our faith and our traditions, we will have used well the time allotted to us. Faced with the prospect of combat, it may be tempting to set aside what we know is right. A high price is paid for such a departure. Others *may* suffer for our lapses; we *always* do. It is an earned privilege to hold your head high.

The other letter is from Jacob L. Devers, The Commanding General of the United States Army. It is dated December 18, 1945.

Dear Lieutenant Howard,

Your recent return to the civilian pursuits which you left at our country's call prompts me to express my sincere appreciation for the service you have rendered the Army Ground Forces.

Our victory would not have been possible without your aid and the aid of other citizens who, like you, left their homes and families to defend our principles of freedom.

The responsibilities of members of a citizen army have not ceased with the termination of hostilities. I know that you realize your duties to your Government as a private citizen all the more as a result of your military experience.

I know too, that you will always remember, with pleasure and just pride, the friendships you have made, your experiences with the finest Army in the world, and the sincere gratitude of our Nation.

That letter, too, represents the civilization that once prevailed in this land, speaking openly and proudly of the responsibilities of the citizens. The remarkable performance of America's military forces in that era was, I am firmly convinced, a reflection of the then reigning culture, in which responsibilities to God, to country, to community, to neighbors, and to family were willingly accepted as the givens of life in this free country.

Americans of that vintage, the college graduates, the day laborers and the housewives had an emotional stability, a sturdiness that could solidly withstand losses, disappointments and frustrations—a common American trait that is all too rare today.

In the World War II speech, it is noted that despite relentless emotional stress, only a very small percentage of the troops in our battalion had psychological breakdowns, or combat fatigue, as it was called, and not many turned to alcohol as an escape mechanism. On November 11, 2010, New York Times columnist Bob Herbert wrote a long column just after the Army psychiatrist Nidal Malik Hasan slaughtered troops at Fort Hood where he was stationed. Herbert reported on "the enormous problem of troops returning from Afghanistan and Iraq with some form of mental disorder. The case loads are off the charts . . . post-traumatic stress disorder or depression, or both, are accompanied by substance abuse, problems with anger management, domestic violence and family breakdown . . ." By the end of the summer, the Army was reporting the highest tally of soldier suicides since accurate record keeping began.

MASSIVE FEDERALLY-FINANCED RESEARCH: THE KISS OF DEATH FOR STUDENT-CENTERED HIGHER EDUCATION

September 2, 1958 marked the beginning of a new era of seismic change even more destructive than the ravages of radicalism, in abolishing the educational philosophy which for two centuries had formed an American populace immensely successful in building the free society.

It was the National Defense Education Act which led to the denaturing of America's schools and colleges. Although President Nicholas Murray Butler had warned the Trustees of New York University in 1921 that the Federal funding of America's schools and colleges would lead to a national catastrophe, and all the concerns he expressed in that warning have since been fulfilled, even he, wise as he was, did not anticipate the one automatically fatal consequence of government-controlled education.

Although Scholarly research had been a feature of university life in Europe through the years, a professor's career in America was predominantly focused on teaching until Johns Hopkins University was founded in Baltimore in 1876. It was modeled after German universities with substantial concentration on research and lab work.

As scientific and technological inventions and discoveries advanced, the role of research on American campuses had grown steadily, but when the door to Federally-funded research opened wide in response to the Sputnik scare, the volume of Federal research multiplied so fast that before long it accounted for more than half the total university budget on many campuses. MORE THAN HALF OF THE UNIVERSITY BUDGET!! In 1962, four years after the counter-Sputnik bill, Harvard's President Pusey issued a formal report about the impact of Federal funding. He observed that the science programs had grown rapidly while programs in other fields had not. The number of faculty members primarily engaged in research had swelled out of all proportion to faculty members who spent their time in what used to be the central purpose of the university, the teaching of students. Similarly, the ratio of new research faculty members to the old-timers who knew the ways and reasons of university policy was increasing. In the same year, President Davidson of the University of Louisville reported that in the eleven years since his institution had inaugurated its first program in doctoral studies, eight new doctoral programs had been developed, all in science and all in response to the availability of federal funds. Soon research was elevated to the highest throne on the university campus, with many research professors receiving the university's top salaries, and the deliberations in faculty councils frequently dominated by the research viewpoint rather than the teaching one.

Research is not education. It is an adjunct of the educational process. Education involves transmitting to students knowledge, principles, traditions, understanding, techniques, and the skills of rational analysis. Education assumes that knowledge has something to teach ignorance, that experience has something to teach inexperience, that informed judgment has something to teach raw judgment, that wisdom is the distillation of what people have learned over time will produce beneficial results or will produce unsuccessful or harmful results. The bedrock principle of education is to prepare the student for a well-ordered and productive life in our free society.

In total contrast, the bedrock principle of research is the assurance of unrestricted study and exploration. You can't tell a researcher, "Yes, do study that subject, but these three aspects of it are foreclosed." That makes no sense at all. It slams the door on progress. The value-free, nonjudgmental principle of research has become totally dominant and now minimizes or suppresses the education principle at university after university. The very definition of education was abolished for most universities and the faculty, rather than the students, became the center of attention.

VALUE—NEUTRAL EDUCATION

In 1969, when the campus turmoil was at its most fevered and destructive, President Nixon appointed A Task Force on Priorities in

Higher Education. The sixteen members included thirteen college and university presidents, a Vice Chancellor for Student and Curricular Affairs and two well-known industrial officers. We went to the White House for our marching orders. The President had a more pressing meeting so his Chief of Staff, Dr. Arthur Burns, explained our mission. The President hoped that our commission could offer advice on how The Government could be helpful in calming things down on the campuses so that higher education could once again focus its attention on our proper work. We were invited to "express our judgment on the whole range of major difficulties facing higher education."

The Committee met several times and all of us were visited by graduate students with tape recorders so we could offer our thoughts on the issues that had been raised. Eventually, we met in the offices of our Chairman, Dr. James Hester, President of New York University. We were given copies of a draft of our report for our perusal. The recommendations included Financial aid for disadvantaged students; Extra fund support for Negro Colleges; Support for Health Care Professional Education; Increased tax incentives for gifts to colleges and universities; Support for high quality graduate and professional education; Observations about institutional self-improvement such as more efficient use of resources and clarification of institutional governance; and finally, the creation of a National Academy of Higher Education, "federally chartered and modeled after the National Academy of Sciences."

When all of us had read the draft, The Chairman asked for comments. All the others approved the text. I raised my hand. "What is it, John?" Dr. Hester asked. I said that I was astonished at the favorable judgment; that it was shameful for us, who represent the nation's colleges and universities, to ignore completely what Dr. Burns had requested of us. "We seem to be fighting a war in Vietnam and the people don't understand why. Students and faculty are especially angry about the matter. The Federal Government must engage in a national campaign to explain what we are up to. We have a bad and increasing problem with the use of illegal drugs on campus and need the government to inform the public about the physical and emotional damage caused by drugs. We have students and other revolutionaries destroying the campuses and we are reluctant to call in the police." We need to know more about the radical organizations that foment the campus turmoil."

There was dead silence. Then one university president said, "But John, all these things involve value judgments, and we can't make policies that involve value judgments!" I responded that they certainly did involve value judgments, but if value judgments are now taboo in academic communities, there is no meaning to the educational process and wisdom has been cancelled. All the others agreed with him. The draft version was adopted with a single dissenting vote, mine. This was 1970.

MEMBERS OF PRESIDENT'S TASK FORCE ON PRIORITIES IN HIGHER EDUCATION

James M. Hester, Chairman
President, New York University

George F. Budd
President, Kansas State College of Pittsburg

James C. Fletcher
President, University of Utah

Luther H. Foster
President, Tuskegee Institute

Alexander Heard
Chancellor, Vanderbilt University

John A. Howard
President, Rockford College

Howard W. Johnson
President, M. I. T.

Edward H. Levi
President, University of Chicago

Sebastian V. Martorana
Vice Chancellor for Two-Year Colleges
State University of New York

Neil H. McElroy
Chairman of the Board
The Procter and Gamble Company

Malcolm C. Moos
President, University of Minnesota

Albert L. Nickerson
Director, Mobil Oil Corporation

Rosemary Park
Vice Chancellor for Academic Planning
University of California, Los Angeles

John E. Sawyer
President, Williams College

Paul E. Waldschmidt
President, University of Portland

John C. Weaver
President, University of Missouri

With The Federal Government playing the role of Senior Partner at the universities and at many colleges, the role of the president of an academic institution has been profoundly changed. Where Federal funds now provide a high percentage of the income, the president must be highly qualified as a Washington lobbyist and skillful in negotiation and maintaining a steady flow of federal funds. There can be no tolerance of mediocre performance in this responsibility.

One inevitable consequence of this requirement is that our nation is bereft of eminent academic leaders who are knowledgeable scholars in the realm of the history of education and educational philosophy and serve as eminent spokesmen about education's responsibility to produce graduates who will be thoughtful, well-informed, affirmative citizens of a free society. Instead, they speak about excellence, diversity, innovation, and the success of their university in pushing back the frontiers of knowledge. Often, when they are questioned about their institution's service in strengthening the free society, they will speak about their continuous search for the truth and remind the questioner that Jesus had stated that the truth shall set you free. In doing so, they don't even know that Jesus' statement was, "If ye continue in my word, then are ye my disciples indeed, and ye shall know the truth and the truth shall make you free." That quote is from the Gospel of John 8:31 and 8:32 and the "then" is italicized in the King James version. What follows are quotations from academic leaders.

PRINCETON UNIVERSITY

My fiftieth reunion at Princeton was in 1993. Our University had been in the news in the days before our arrival. President Shapiro had announced that the campus equivalent of the United Way was withdrawing the Boy Scouts from the list of recipients because of its policy of refusing to permit homosexuals to serve as scout masters.

It was pro forma for the university president to speak at our class banquet. When he finished, a number of hands were raised. A good many of our classmates had been active in the Boy Scouts. The first person called upon asked, "Why are we giving the Boy Scouts a hard time?" There was some applause.

President Shapiro replied, "Gentlemen! Gentlemen! You were bright enough to be admitted to this fine university. Surely, you are bright enough to know that change is the nature of things. If your university doesn't change to adjust to new circumstances, it cannot hope to hold its place among the nation's finest academic institutions."

God and eternal truths had been cancelled.

The next morning I went to the President's office and asked to have a brief visit with him, explaining I was there for my 50th reunion and that I had served as the president of two colleges. The secretary said he was extremely busy with reunions and his day was overscheduled. I told her I understood that situation and wondered if I could see his assistant. At her office, I was greeted cordially by an attractive young woman. After a little visit I said I imagined the President anticipated flack about the Boy Scout thing. She said, "Of course, but don't worry about it. It will go away."

I told her that an interesting thing had happened at our banquet. At each place there were plates and cups and napkins handsomely emblazoned with Princeton's Great Seal. Upon it was inscribed the

University Motto—"Dei Sub Numine Viget"—It Flourishes Under The Will of God. I said I understand that the motto takes precedence over all other policies, and asked, "Whose idea of God is Princeton flourishing under these days? Both the Christian and Judaic faiths have strictures limiting sexual activity to married couples."

She said that was an interesting thought and let it go at that. We conversed a bit more and I got up to leave. She came over, put her hand on my shoulder and said, "Thank you for caring so much you unburdened yourself to me." By the time I got back to Illinois, I had calmed down some, so I mailed her materials from our Center on Family, Religion and Society including one commentary which explained that sexual liberation and the family are mutually exclusive. The more there is of the one, the less there will be of the other. There was no acknowledgement from her, so after a while I wrote to ask if she received what I sent her. She wrote that she had, but it didn't interest her at all. Dialogue had already been supplanted in 1993 by political correctness.

On September 13, 2009, Princeton President Shirley Tilghman gave her welcoming speech to entering freshmen. "Taking my cue from David Letterman, I enumerated for newly matriculated freshmen the top ten things I believe they should do before they graduate." Her first bit of advice was, "Call, e-mail, text or IM home, but not too often. As hard as it is for parents to accept, we did not admit them to Princeton when we admitted you. The next four years will mark the final stage in your transition from adolescence to adulthood, and now it's time for you to strike out on your own and make your own decisions. You will surely make mistakes—everyone does—but you will also learn from them."[25]

This was an ill-conceived and most unfortunate recommendation. The family is the oldest human institution and the most important one. In 1948, The United Nations formalized its complete support of the family when it adopted the Universal Declaration of Human Rights. Article I, Section 16 asserts "Men and women of full age without any limitation due to race, nationality or religion have a right to marry and found a family." Section 3, Article 1 states, "The family is the natural unit of society and is entitled to protection by the society and the state."

---

[25] Princeton Alumni Weekly, President's Page, October 7, 2009.

The benefits to the child raised in a natural family have been incontrovertibly established by innumerable studies. The child raised by his or her married mother and father is far more likely than children raised in any other circumstances to succeed in school, in a job and in a marriage, and far less likely to use illegal drugs, commit a crime, run away from home, have emotional problems, become an alcoholic or commit suicide. The family is the most effective breeding ground for the good life and the good society.

When I entered Princeton in 1939, President Harold Dodds wrote to my parents: "We will do our utmost to guide him so that he will emerge a useful, responsible member of society. We count on your assistance, believing that the influence of the home should not end at the college door."

Dr. Lewis Mayhew

In his address as the new President of the American Association of Higher Education in July of 1969, Dr. Lewis Mayhew said, "Colleges are not churches, clinics, or even parents. Whether or not a student burns a draft card, participates in a civil rights march, engages in pre-marital or extra-marital sexual activity, becomes pregnant, attends church, sleeps all day or drinks all night, is not really the concern of an educational institution."

Yale University

On August 31, 1981, A. Bartlett Giamatti, the President of Yale University, gave a speech to the entering freshman entitled, "A Liberal Education and the New Coercion."

In introducing Yale's definition of a liberal education, he asks several rhetorical questions one of which is, "Is it an education pursued, as Cardinal Newman believed, in a spirit that studies a subject simply for and in itself, without concern for the practical consequences of such a study? That would be a description of the proper attitude to bring to your studies."

Without concern for the practical consequences of such a study! Such an attitude would cut the student loose from any obligations to the society. Indeed, that attitude is an outright rejection of Aristotle's dictum . . .

> I have said what I believe because there are now in America powerful voices which attack and will continue to attack these very ideas.
>
> A self-proclaimed "Moral Majority," and its satellite or client groups, cunning in the use of a native blend of old intimidation and new technology, threaten the values I have named. Angry at change, rigid in the application of chauvinistic slogans, absolutistic in morality, they threaten through political pressure or public denunciation whoever dares to disagree with their authoritarian positions. Using television, direct mail and economic boycott, they would sweep before them anyone who holds a different opinion."

His tirade against "dangerous malicious nonsense" continues to grow more intense and more vindictive as he continues. It is an illustration of the concept of education, although an intemperate one, that was espoused by the members of President Nixon's Task Force on Priorities in Higher Education.

Harvard University

The May-June 1988 issue of the Harvard Magazine, published an eleven page-essay, "Ethics, The University and Society" by President Derek Bok. He observes that revelations about the conduct of many influential Americans have caused wide concern about standards of behavior and have become a national concern . . . "At a deeper level, one can detect a parallel shift in the attitudes of the American people. During most of the twentieth century, first artists and intellectuals; then broader segments of the society, challenged every convention, every prohibition, every regulation that cramped the human spirit, or blocked its appetites and ambitions. Today, a reaction has set in, born of a recognition that the public needs common standards to hold a diverse society together . . . Religious institutions no longer seem as able as they once were to impart basic values to the young . . . Such studies as we have about the values of college students only heighten these concerns. Several studies have found that undergraduates are growing less altruistic and more preoccupied with self-serving goals . . . .

"The Older Tradition" is the subtitle for an extensive history of the centuries during which character education was the central goal of the university experience—"The President, professors and tutors of the University at Cambridge . . . shall exert their best endeavors to impress on the minds of youth committed to their care and instruction the principles of piety, and justice, and a sacred regard for truth, love of their country, humanity, and universal benevolence, sobriety, industry and frugality, chastity, moderation and temperance, and those other virtues which are the ornament of human society and the basis on which a republican constitution is founded." This is quoted from a Massachusetts law enacted in 1789 and reaffirmed in 1826.

Bok quotes an early President of Yale, Noah Porter, "The most efficient of all moral influences in a college are those which proceed from the personal characters of the instructors."

Another segment of his analysis is entitled "The Decline of Moral Instruction." President Bok lists a number of forces that have downgraded the primary attention to the students' character: the influence of Darwin's Origin of Species; the transition to research universities; the change from a largely rural and small town student body to a much more metropolitan one; the new attitudes of many different ethnic groups; the cancellation of the university's "in loco parentis" role; a new unconcern for the personal character of faculty members; and the cancellation of many university rules of student conduct.

The last seven pages are basically a lament. "The American nation is greatly in need of some means to civilize new generations of the people, preparing them to serve as honest, benevolent, productive citizens of a free society, and all of Harvard's deliberations and studies and initiatives and earnest concerns have not resulted in any effective means of Character Education."

Dr. Bok's conclusion:

> Despite the importance of moral development to the individual and the society, one cannot say that higher education has demonstrated a deep concern for the problem. Some efforts are being made on every

> campus, and a number of religious institutions and small independent colleges actually devote much time and energy to the task. More often, however, and especially at large universities, the subject is not treated as a serious responsibility worthy of sustained discussion, and determined action by the faculty and administration. Let me add that Harvard has not done all that it should . . . If this situation is to change, there is no doubt where the initiative must lie. Universities will never do much to encourage a genuine concern for ethical issues or to help their students to acquire a strong and carefully considered set of moral values until presidents and deans take the lead."

The Miami Herald of February 9, 1969, carried an Associated Press story that "Harvard had cancelled a course in Riot Control apparently in response to Negro objections. The Negroes opposed any assistance in suppressing riots because they are one of the few instruments of power available to black people in this political system."

INVENTORY OF UNIVERSITY GOALS

In 1968, The American Council on Education published a book entitled University Goals and Academic Power which reported on a study about the purposes of American universities. A questionnaire had been sent to 10,000 faculty members and administrators at 68 universities. More than 7000 usable responses were received. The participants were asked what are the purposes of your university, rated according to the order of importance? And what do you think should be the purposes, also rated by order of importance?

The number one purpose, by a wide margin, was, "Protecting the Faculty's Right to Academic Freedom." That was also the number one choice among the respondents as to what should be most important. The number two goal was "Increase or maintain the prestige of the university;" number three was "Maintain top quality in those programs felt to be especially important;" number four was, "Ensure the continued confidence and support of those who contribute substantially to the finances and other material resource needs of the university;" number five was, "Keep up to date and responsive;" number six was, "Train students in methods of scholarship and/or scientific research and/or creative endeavor;" and number seven was "Carry on pure research."

Professor Gross and Dean Grambsch note a remarkable characteristic of the ratings is "that only one of the seven top goals is concerned in any way with the students, and that one—the goal of training students for research and scholarship—is closely related to the scholarly interests of professors and with the emphasis given to pure research. The singular scarcity of student-oriented goals in the top group is all the more startling when one considers that 18 of the 47 goals listed in the questionnaire refer directly to the students. Apparently the current complaint that universities give little attention to the interests of the students has considerable basis in fact . . .

In general, we may say that American universities emphasize the faculty's academic freedom, concern themselves primarily with goals relating to pure research and with maintaining or enhancing the university's position, and manifest relatively little interest in the student beyond developing his scholarly ability."[26]

The rapid entry of the U.S. Government into the formulation and control of American schooling, following the launching of Sputnik, introduced a whole new set of complications and serious problems into the educational enterprise with major decisions made by a Congress which already had assumed more responsibilities than it could possibly deliver on intelligently.

In the summer of 1980, we published a commentary about the condition of American education which we hoped would be useful to whomever was elected president that year. The advice it offered seems as pertinent today as it did thirty years ago. What follows is a slightly abbreviated version of it.

---

[26] Edward Gross and Paul V Grambsch, University Goals and Academic Power, American Council on Education, Washington DC, 1968, pp. 30, 31.

EDUCATION IN AMERICA: A MEMORANDUM FOR THE U.S. PRESIDENT IN THE EIGHTIES

by John A. Howard

Mr. President:

I am pleased to invite your attention to the subject of the American educational system. May I suggest that, with the sole exception of religion, schooling is the foremost long-range determinant of the well-being of the nation.

In determining government's part in education, you, Sir, are less fortunate than most of your predecessors, for in seeking advice, you will discover a virtual absence of towering figures within the educational profession who speak knowledgeably and forthrightly about the purposes of the schools and colleges. Predictably, our recently appointed First Secretary of Education, Shirley Hufstedler, began an interview with the statement, "My first priority is to set the Department of Education on a foundation of excellence."[27]

Excellence without a context has no meaning. Fagin was an excellent teacher of pickpockets. This mindless assertion is typical of many college presidents who avoid speaking of the purpose of education by claiming diversity, innovation, extending the limits of man's knowledge and excellence as favorable attributes of their institutions. It is a dramatic and disquieting symbol of the academic preoccupation with the mechanics of education that this choice to be the first Secretary of Education had almost no professional training nor professional experience in the field

---

[27] Arthur Siddon, "Giving Education a New Federal Home," Chicago Tribune Magazine, March 16, 1980, p. 32.

of education. And this confusion of priorities is underscored by the almost total absence of criticism from the academic community about her appointment.

In these circumstances, it seems useful to look back to the educational leadership of earlier times for understanding and guidance. In 1952, President Gordon Keith Chalmers of Kenyon College presented his concept of schooling for a free society in a volume entitled, The Republic and the Person.[28] As the title suggests, the author has taken into account the eternal tension between the rights and desires of the individual on the one hand and, on the other, the obligations imposed upon the individual by his membership in the national society. In a free nation, this is the one absolutely necessary focus for the schools and colleges. The individual citizen must be helped to reach a proper and affirmative accommodation between rightful self-interest and rightful public interest. All other considerations are subordinate to this. If pursuit of private interest is not carried on within a framework of personal commitment to lawfulness, ethics and other codes protecting the well-being of the group, then the nation can easily become fragmented into pressure groups, each demanding that its parochial interests be served at the expense of others. In the United States this process has advanced so far that the government veers one direction and then another as various coalitions of militant interest groups wax and wane. Strikes, demonstrations, passion and power tactics are supplanting principle and rationality. We are moving toward government by decibel.

Throughout his analysis, Dr. Chalmers stresses his concern that the system of education must produce effective citizens. Consider several of his observations:

> "The general object of education has become more and more to *condition the mass attitude toward specific social improvements*, and enthusiasm for these reforms has diverted energy from the ancient and central task of converting the reason—of converting it from the knowledge and love of what is mean to the knowledge and love of what is worthy."[29] [Emphasis added.]

---

[28] Gordon Keith Chalmers, The Republic and the Person, Henry Regnery Company, 1952.

[29] Ibid., p. 7.

> "It is altogether possible that despite the fanfare of postwar reform the American educational system will continue to promote moral adolescence. That is the first danger of the present, the danger most pertinent to society and politics and most appropriate to be dealt with by education. For the proper object of school and college is moral maturity."[30]

Obviously, Mr. President, you cannot personally or officially lead the educational profession out of its preoccupation with the mechanics of schooling and its entrenched indifference to the preparation of the students for responsible citizenship, but you do, Sir, need to understand how the federal government's role in education has fortified that indifference and, worse, contributed extensively to the rising level of unjust, irrational and unethical conduct within the educational system. The governmental mechanisms that have evolved in the attempt to finance and improve education are, themselves, in many instances, corruptive and need to be revised or abolished.

The United States Department of Education will be spending $13.5 billion in fiscal 1981.[31] Let us consider some of the negative consequences of this torrent of help.

Leadership

John D. Millett, one of the senior analysts of educational governance, writes, "I want to emphasize . . . that leadership is the indispensable ingredient for the determination of purpose and for the accomplishment of desired ends,"[32] and he calls attention to the insistence of Princeton's former president, Harold W. Dodds, that "the prime function of the president should be to serve as an educational leader."[33]

It was noted earlier that there is a scarcity of academic executives noted for their commentaries on the purposes of education. This dearth is, to some extent, a consequence of the kind of federal assistance

30 Ibid., pp. 254, 255.

31 The Budget of the United States Government, pp. 434-435.

32 John D. Millett, Strengthening Community in Higher Education, Academy for Educational Development, 1974, p. v.

33 Ibid., p. 50.

which has been provided. It will become evident in later sections of this analysis that the time and attention of the academic president has been increasingly pre-empted by the demands and the special problems of being a dependent of the federal government and an agent for the accomplishment of goals it has imposed on the academic community. At this point, let us examine how a dependence on research revenues has affected the qualifications that are sought in the academic leadership.

Historically, most of the academic presidents who were renowned for their educational philosophy were heads of major universities since those universities had the resources and the prestige to attract able people and their spokesmen have always been able to command the public ear. Today the stature of the major universities is determined largely by their respective capacities to attract eminent research scholars, and the federal government is the preponderant source of funds for academic research. Thus a major university would be ill-advised to consider any candidate for its presidency who would not be effective in sustaining and increasing the flow of federal research dollars. It is a most unusual individual who can fit President Dodd's requirement that the president be primarily an educational leader involving himself in the rationale and the implementation of educational programs on his campus, and at the same time be a highly visible mover and shaker in the Washington circles where priorities for research grants are determined.

Indeed the concept of the university leader envisioned by Dr. Dodds has all but passed from the American scene, and most university faculties nowadays would be startled, if not outraged, by any initiatives of the president to involve himself in curricular deliberations. The changes which have resulted in the removal of the most eminent academic officers from the realm of educational theory and curriculum reform have impoverished the entire educational function in America.

THE PURPOSES OF EDUCATION

During the 1930's and 1940's the centuries-old view that education's primary purpose was to form the moral character of the citizens was subject to increasing pressure from new concepts and philosophies. As Douglas Sloan has noted, "The growing force of scientific naturalism . . . began . . . to bias the outcome . . . more toward subjectivism, toward ethical relativism, toward functionalism, toward moral determinism."[34] These views of man and society rejected the traditional concepts of right and wrong on which the institutions of American society operated. As these antitraditional views gained strength in the academic community, thoughtful leadership on the campuses became concerned about how they were skewing the educational process. President James Conant of Harvard University appointed a committee of eminent scholars to study this matter. After two years of deliberation, the committee report was published in 1945 under the title, General Education in a Free Society.[35] It reasserted the need for common moral and social values in the society and reaffirmed education's responsibility to concern itself with these values.

In this conflict of concepts about the nature of man and society and the consequent role of education, the traditional view was still dominant, at least in the *policies* of colleges and universities, when the research function was propelled into a commanding position on the campuses by the outpouring of federal grants. The atmosphere of *value neutrality* required for research work is hardly conducive to any rational and intentional educational program to prepare the students for the responsibilities of living in a free society.

As research activities burgeoned on the campuses and the research scholars became the academic elite and their primary activity was wholly in harmony with the rising tide of ethical relativism in the social sciences, the stage was set for the collapse of the ancient view of the purposes of education. Value neutrality had triumphed. The definition of research had supplanted the definition of education. There was no longer any justifiable basis for *institutional* policies to govern the moral content of the educational program or the behavior of the individuals engaged in the educational process. The zealot preaching political revolution or moral anarchy had become eligible to teach in the classroom, speak from an academic platform or organize a revolutionary group on campus. The students were given to understand that one point of view was just as welcome as any other and, *as far as the university was officially concerned*, it made no difference which views the student adopted for himself on any subject.

---

34 Sloan, op. cit. p. 27.

35 General Education in a Free Society, Report of the Harvard Committee, Harvard University Press, 1945.

The authority of knowledge as a guide for human conduct was jettisoned on one campus after another in the rush to embrace the "new enlightenment." And then, what was there left for academic officers to say about their educational programs other than safely neutral and meaningless mouthings about excellence and innovation? As this change, which started with the prestigious institutions, became the orthodoxy in higher education, it was only a matter of time before the value-neutral concepts began to contaminate the high schools and elementary schools as well.

The avalanche of federal research funds had tipped the balance in favor of a new philosophy of education with unanticipated, unintended and disquieting consequences.

INTEGRITY AND OTHER CASUALITIES OF VALUE NEUTRALITY

When the doors were opened for the forthright advocacy of radical social, economic, political and educational change, the dissidents quickly occupied center stage on campus and, to a large extent, still occupy it. The people who are dissatisfied with the status quo will always agitate for a new order to the extent that such agitation is permitted. Since the new policies were not only hospitable to the polemics of change and revolution, but also had dispensed with the curricular espousal of the traditions, standards and institutions of the American society, the dissidents were often without effective opposition or rebuttal in the academic forums. The large body of faculty members that believed in the American civilization were not on campus to fight a counterrevolution. They went about their daily work and devoted their leisure time to their families and other private interests. In these circumstances, the revolutionary counterculture took root and burgeoned all out of proportion to the percentage of campus adults sympathetic to its reasons and intentions.

The students found themselves in a strange environment. Never before had a whole generation of Americans come to adulthood in circumstances where there was no consensus as to behavioral limitations and obligations. It was at first a heady experience for the young, but it turned out also to be a deeply disturbing experience for the bright and sensitive ones. If nothing is generally held to be inherently right or wrong, good or bad, then no direction is forward and it is impossible to develop a sense of direction in one's life, or to have a sense of self-esteem. The yardsticks for measuring one's worth are scuttled along with the values. Psychologically, the human being cannot withstand a permanent milieu of value neutrality. Thus, it was that the students became tragically vulnerable to the lure of madmen and demagogues of every flavor who proclaimed that *they did know what was the good life*. The circumstances were propitious for the rise of cultism of every sort—drug cults, revolutionary cults, religious cults, pastoral communes, witchcraft, mysticism and cults of travel to exotic places. How many promising young lives were laid waste by the no-right no-wrong ambience of the campus can only be guessed at.

The deterioration of conduct on the school grounds and the college campuses has been rapid and pervasive. Last year two prestigious educational bodies issued reports on this matter. The American Assembly of Columbia University, in its pamphlet, "The Integrity of Higher Education," listed many examples of unethical conduct including, "plagiarism by both teachers and students; exploitation by faculty and administrators of graduate students and teaching assistants; 'double-dipping' by academic professionals from several grant sources for the same labors performed; . . . grade inflation and unwarranted recommendations for students; and the unjustified imposition of prerequisites."[36]

The Carnegie Council on Policy Studies in Higher Education is more comprehensive in its review of the declining integrity of the campuses. Some of the categories judged to be of greatest concern were: "A significant and apparently increasing amount of cheating by students in academic assignments; a substantial misuse by students of public financial aid; theft and destruction by students of valuable property, most specifically library books and journals; inflation of grades by faculty members; . . . inflated and misleading advertising by some institutions in search for students."[37]

The documentation of these concerns is even more disquieting than their mere listing. One study is cited in which 42% of the students

---

[36] "The Integrity of Higher Education," The American Assembly of Columbia University, 1979, p. 5.

[37] Fair Practices in Higher Education, Report of the Carnegie Council on Policy Studies in Higher Education, Jossey Bass Publishers, 1979, p. 3.

in one of the most highly regarded liberal-arts colleges admitted to having cheated on a paper or examination. Three major universities were reported to have annual losses by theft of 4 or 5 percent of the books in their undergraduate libraries. Imagine the cost of replacing half the library collection every ten or twelve years! Perhaps the most dismaying statistic of all comes from a major survey the Carnegie Council had conducted in 1975 in which "Sixty-one percent of the undergraduates responding . . . believed it was possible to get good grades without really understanding the material."[38] How far has the deterioration advanced?

At the precollege level, matters may be even worse. In a survey conducted by the Chicago Teachers Union, 48 percent of the 3800 respondents said they had been victims of a school-related crime or attempted crime, and sixty percent of them had been victimized more than once.[39] Emery Stoops, a professor emeritus of educational administration and supervision, has offered an overview of school problems in an article "The Blackboard Jungle Has Become a Reality."

> "Every month, 5,000 teachers are attacked in schools, something is stolen from one of every nine students, and one out of every four school buildings is vandalized . . . .
>
> The Senate Subcommittee to Investigate Juvenile Delinquency reported that vandalism costs this country more than a half-billion dollars per year . . .
>
> Drug abuse has thrust itself into the total curriculum at the rate of more than ten percent per year—that means an increase of 90 percent since 1970!"[40]

In addition to the unanticipated encouragement of the value-neutral philosophy provided by the massive support for the research function, the government has contributed substantially to the breakdown of the integrity of education in other unintended ways. The enormous

---

38 Ibid., p. 27.

39 Casey Banas, "50% of Teachers Victims of Crime, Survey Reports," Chicago Tribune, October 7, 1979.

40 Emery Stoops, "The Blackboard Jungle Has Become a Reality," Human Events, November 17, 1979, p. 14.

programs of funding have strengthened the utopian notion that the government *owes* the citizens comprehensive and perpetual support, and the very magnitude of the bureaucracy which administers the programs has a rigidity and an incapacity to cope with local circumstances which cause injustices and protect dishonesty. Melvin E. Clark, the director of student financial aid at Adams State College, explains these problems:

> "We are angry with the 'something for nothing' syndrome that affects many of our students. They want free money, free grades, and a degree that they will not work to earn.
>
> We are angry with the federal and state laws, rules and regulations that would deny us the flexibility to seek out and eliminate the freeloader and the fraud.
>
> We are angry with federal and state administrators that will not recognize the damage being done to the total financial-assistance program by students defaulting on loans and declaring bankruptcy and, by their very inaction, perpetuating the continued rip-off of the defenseless taxpayer . . .
>
> We are angry with a needs-analysis system, developed with the blessing of the federal government, that would establish a cost-of-living budget for independent students with families greater than the salaries we can offer our junior professionals."[41]

Several months ago, columnist Bill Raspberry wrote about the student-loan situation. "Loans from commercial sources are taken seriously. Loans from the government—from you and me—are shrugged off as of no particular importance. The situation has reached the point that student-loan defaults now total more than $2 billion."[42]

Permit me, Sir, a personal anecdote which dramatizes the unintentional but inexorable corruptive force of the federal government's role in education. During the last few years that I served as a college

---

41 Melvin E. Clark, "Financial Aid Officers Are Angry Too," College Board Review, Summer 1977, p. 25.

42 Bill Raspberry, "Defaulted Student Loans Mount Up," Chicago Tribune, September 18, 1979.

president, one of the pleasant annual occurrences was a visit from a young man who was a field agent for the national headquarters of one of the major church bodies. His work was to visit student organizations affiliated with his church on various campuses offering advice and encouragement and taking recommendations back to headquarters about how to provide more effective support for the campus constituencies. He also solicited, in a thoughtful and friendly fashion, the support of campus administrators for the activities of his affiliated student groups.

The last time he came by, he dispensed with the usual pleasantries and said that he faced a critical difficulty and needed advice. It seems that the federal government, in the enthusiasm for one of its equal-opportunities programs, had sent a directive to the nation's campuses requiring that all student groups that were formally recognized by the college submit an affidavit that their membership was open to anyone on campus. This was an impossible obligation for the student groups under his guidance because they were restricted to communicants of his church denomination, and the members all participated in the conduct of their worship services. On each of the half dozen campuses he had recently visited, the students were uncertain about what to do, so that he as their agent had visited with deans and ombudspersons seeking their help in resolving the dilemma. In each case, he had been advised to have the student group simply sign the affidavit and not fret about it, since it was unlikely that outsiders would want to participate. "In other words," said he, "the official counsel was that our students should engage in intentional and formalized deceit. My objections to that advice were brushed aside as petty self-righteousness, in the category of a nuisance."

Mr. President, this homely little drama, which so far as I know has not been properly resolved, brings into focus the stark and devastating shortcomings inherent in the federal subsidy and regulation of the educational function. The government is a political instrumentality responding to the ebb and flow of political forces and public passions. When the public pressure to bring about change reaches an intolerable level, the government responds to that pressure through its mechanisms without regard to the nature or the purposes of the activities on which those mechanisms impinge. Thus as the educational system has become financially dependent upon the central government, the government has used that financial captivity to impose on the schools and colleges policies and requirements dictated by political expediency which have variously restricted, corrupted and denatured the educational system. In this instance, the heavy yoke of government has reduced college officers to advocating dishonesty to their students as the convenient if not the only way to fulfill their obligations.

We will cite other examples of the distorting and corrupting effect of federal legislation, but for now let us amplify on government's effect upon the religious element of American education.

RELIGION, STEP TO THE REAR OF THE BUS!

Even among the nation's private educational institutions, the role of religion has been diminished by the federal funding of education. The difficulty is that given the separation of church and state, as state moves in, church must move out. This cause and effect was brought into focus in a court case in Maryland in the early 1960's wherein some citizens sued the state for distributing funds to church-related colleges, charging that this was an unconstitutional allocation of public monies. The court found that in the case of some of the recipient institutions, the relationship to the church was so meager that there was no problem, but that the others had a religious character and therefore were improper recipients of government funds. It then became a problem for church-related colleges and universities across the country to determine how much church they had to get rid of in order to remain eligible for government subsidy. Many renowned religious universities reconstituted their boards of trustees so that clergymen would not be in the majority. Some institutions severed the church tie altogether.

The diminishing influence of religion in the private sector of education is manifest in the councils and the formal analyses within the academic profession. In 1975, when the American Academy of Arts and Sciences devoted two issues of its journal, Daedalus, to the status, the purposes and problems and the future of higher education, the subject of religion scarcely found its way into the text of the articles of almost a hundred contributing authors.

The declining importance of religion in the private sector of higher education was even more dramatically reflected in the Report of a Task Force of the National Council of Independent Colleges and

Universities. Entitled, A National Policy for Private Higher Education, the fifty-page text scrupulously avoids any mention of religion, except in one legal citation. The thrust of the report is a plea for more federal subsidy and to that end great care is taken not to give offense to the politically influential public institutions. "In making this case, there is no implication that private higher education as such is in any way superior to public higher education. No invidious comparisons are needed or intended. Both sectors serve important public purposes and both have the capacity for excellence in discharging their functions . . . . A special case must be made for private higher education simply because it is in jeopardy and because new public policies are needed to preserve the benefits accruing from the dual system."[43]

Private higher education has the constitutional privilege of making religion a vital part of the educational experience of its students. At the pre-college level, this is regarded by vast numbers of citizens as the most important justification for creating and sustaining private schools with tuition and gifts. It is a matter worthy of long and careful thought, Mr. President, that this largest and most prestigious organization of private colleges has chosen the course of sacrificing religion in order to get a larger volume of federal subsidy. It is certain that many institutional members of this body still proudly look upon the religious nature of their educational programs as superior to what public institutions are permitted to offer their students, but these views are now being squeezed out by the dismal economic circumstances of academia and the present federal policies of funding for education. This is an ominous trend for any nation unless it is prepared to declare for paganism.

THE DEVASTATION CAUSED BY IMPOSING POLITICAL GOALS UPON THE EDUCATIONAL SYSTEM

> ". . . qualities which may be virtues in politics can be vices for scholarship, and the other way around. The fashionable political virtues reflected in the new regulators' directives are bent upon achieving an egalitarian society which is simultaneously a humane

---

43 A National Policy for Private Higher Education, Report of a Task Force of the National Council of Independent Colleges and Universities, Association of American Colleges, 1974, p. 9.

> society and an environmentally risk-free society. Universities, as well as business firms, are deemed to be vessels within which these admirable goals are to be achieved under the close scrutiny of public officials . . . . what is required of the university is that it assign to such a social role a priority which directly conflicts with essential and central tasks."[44]

This is part of the concluding statement by Professor Paul Seabury in a recent volume of essays about the relationship between the universities and the federal government. It describes forthrightly a category of problems which Washington has imposed on the schools as well as the colleges, problems that are gravely distorting and damaging the educational process. This failure of governmental judgment is all the more grievous because it involves issues that are so sensitive that most educators as well as politicians are fearful of even raising them publicly, knowing that there will be little chance for facts and rationality even to be heard amid the clamor of passions they will generate. Still, what hope is there for the nation if its leaders cannot bring themselves to reconsider policies which have had extensive unanticipated destructive consequences?

Certain efforts by the federal government to improve and equalize educational opportunities for minority groups have produced far more harm than benefit. Consider, for instance, the process of busing students for the specific purpose of achieving racial integration. If youngsters are transported daily from the inner city to some more affluent region of the city, what are the inevitable consequences? The parents of the inner-city children will find it exceedingly difficult to work directly with the remote teachers, to give the extra psychological support to the children placed in this disadvantageous circumstance. The teachers in a school thus integrated face awesome new burdens. How can they conduct classes composed of two culturally disparate groups, and serve either one well? Even if the income levels of the two groups are not significantly different, the vocabulary and the illustrations which will speak most effectively to one group are not likely to do so equally

---

[44] Bureaucrats and Brainpower, ed. Paul Seabury, Institute for Contemporary Studies, 1979, pp. 149-150.

well for the other. From the perspective of the educational function, the commendable intention of the busing-for-integration policy is fundamentally counterproductive in practice. It harms most the very people it is intended to benefit, and it harms the other students as well. If the government's intent is genuinely to improve the educational experience of the inner-city students, far better to take some of the money now squandered in busing and distribute it as salary premiums above the salary schedule to the teachers and administrators serving the inner-city schools. Those students need teachers with special training and extra talents, and such premiums would help to recruit a more capable staff where it is needed most.

At the college level, there is a counterproductivity of comparable magnitude in the policies of affirmative action. Here it is necessary to clarify the terminology. The phrase "affirmative action" is now sometimes used as synonymous with programs to assure equal job opportunities. That is a blurring of two concepts that were altogether different at the time they became designations for governmental activities. When the equal-opportunities program was developed as an aspect of the government's contractual relationships, the only objective was to try to ensure that no qualified individual would be denied a job or employment privileges because of his race, religion or national origin. Merit alone was to be the determinant. The equality that was sought was equality among individuals capable of fulfilling the responsibilities of a specific position.

Affirmative action introduced the concept of compensatory consideration for groups that had not fared well in the job market. It involved the subordination of job qualifications to other concerns in the government's regulation of the contractor's employment policies. This, then, was the original distinction between federal programs of equal opportunities and federal programs of affirmative action. The one focused on a fair chance for all qualified candidates, the other insisted that other concerns should take precedence. This differentiation has become blurred by semantics. It is obvious that various social, cultural, political and economic factors diminish the chances that blacks, Puerto Ricans and other segments of the population will have the kind of schooling and other preparatory experiences that qualify them for the preferred jobs. Thus, to speak of equal job opportunities only for those who are well trained is not to speak of equal job opportunities for all citizens, but only for a favored segment of the citizens. It is perhaps out of recognition of this circumstance that the phrase "equal job opportunities" has jumped the fence and become the equivalent of affirmative action.

The nation's consideration of this issue will have a better chance of resulting in a realistic and workable outcome if we re-establish the distinction between opportunities available according to merit and opportunities created to assist the less qualified. That differentiation will permit us to acknowledge the validity of the concern reflected in both programs, to recognize the general practicality of equal job opportunity policies, and to examine and evaluate affirmative action as a technique and assess the damage which obligatory affirmative action has inflicted upon the society.

Let us consider some of the damage. In the first place, when any factor other than the skill to do the job is imposed as the primary determinant in the policies which regulate hiring and promotion, the whole fabric of employment relationships is strained and torn. In October 1974, Estelle Fishbein, the special assistant attorney general for the University of Maryland, identified a number of distressing consequences which affirmative action had already produced in the academic community. In a speech at the annual conference of the American Council on Education, she noted that the fear of losing government contracts and the fear of becoming the subject of affirmative-action lawsuits had an intimidating impact upon administrative and faculty officers, and was skewing their personnel decisions with serious disruptive consequences. In their zeal to comply with affirmative action requirements, academic institutions were bidding frantically against each other for scarce candidates from the favored categories, sometimes offering faculty rank and salary vastly disproportionate to the candidate's credentials. Such preferential treatment of minority and women candidates grievously undermines both the morale and the cooperative relationships of the faculty. Among other problems which she cited was the increasing frequency with which legal counsel had to be consulted prior to making the operating decisions of the academic institution. Carrying that point further, it must be noted that in addition to the rising dollar cost of the legal services, the price paid by the university includes delayed decisions, an inhibition on program initiatives and even a growing reluctance to accept administrative responsibilities. It will be recognized that these particular effects combined with a reduction in the competence of the teaching staff, and a sagging morale constitute an ominous erosion of the central activity of the academic institution.[45]

What about the impact of affirmative action upon the individual and the groups granted preferential treatment under the policy? There seems to be no doubt that there has been an increase in the number and percentage of minorities and women included in the work force and appointed to positions of major responsibility, although the increases in the latter are not overwhelming, but there are long-range negative effects of affirmative action that may far outweigh the gains. There is certainly a rekindling of group prejudice among the white males and their families who perceive that they have been foreclosed from employment, enrollment or advancement opportunities as a result of governmental policies. It would be a sad irony if this should reach a dimension to reverse the trend of intergroup amity which has been one of the few major triumphs of our nation in recent decades.

Another distressing aspect of the negative consequences was set forth in an article in the Southwestern University Law Review, by Lina A. Groglia.

> "Many members of preferred groups who do not require preferential treatment . . . vigorously object to it. For example, the eminent [black] economist, Thomas Sowell, has written: 'What all the arguments and campaigns for quotas are really saying, loud and clear, is that *black people just don't have it*, and that they will have to be given something in order to have something. The devastating impact of this message on black people—particularly black young people—will outweigh any few extra jobs that may result from this strategy. Those black people who are already competent . . . will be completely undermined, as black becomes synonymous—in the minds of black and white alike—with incompetence,

45 In March of 1978, the University of Chicago arrived at an affirmative-action agreement with HEW, after weeks of intensive negotiations. The Chicago Tribune offered an editorial comment that it is a "maddening waste of public and private resources as institutions far better administered than the federal government are required to prove their innocence with elaborate statistics."

> and black achievement becomes synonymous with charity or payoffs.'"[46]

A further dimension of the price paid by the favored groups was set forth powerfully and poignantly in an autobiographical essay of Richard Rodriguez, published in a periodical called Politicks. Having graduated from Stanford and taken a master's degree at Columbia, he was completing his Ph.D. in Renaissance Literature at Berkeley, and was deluged with extraordinarily lucrative job offers from academic institutions all over the country. He acknowledged that he had indicated he was Hispanic-American on the applications for student financial aid. "It didn't really occur to me," he wrote, "to say anything else . . . Thus I complied with and encouraged the odd bureaucratic logic of affirmative action. My progress was monitored by Health, Education and Welfare statisticians: my presence was noted each fall by a university public-affairs officer. As I pursued advanced literary studies and learned the skill of reading Spencer, Wordsworth and Emerson, I would hear myself numbered among the disadvantaged." Later in the article, he records the bitter words of a fellow student whose job prospects were as desperate as Rodriguez's were abundant. "I'll bet our records are just about equal," said his friend. "But when we look for jobs this year, it's a different story. You get all the breaks . . . You're a Chicano, and I'm a Jew . . . There isn't any way for me to compete with you. Once there were quotas to keep my parents out of certain schools; now there are quotas to get you in, and the effect on me is the same as it was for them."[47] Richard Rodriguez ultimately decided not to enter the teaching profession. His article is worthy of careful study by anyone trying to evaluate the usefulness of affirmative action. Among the additional points he makes is the error of the assumption that he could be useful in teaching underprivileged members of his own group. As he stressed, "his group," the one he had become qualified to serve, was not the Chicanos, but students accustomed to the academic culture.

Affirmative action, I submit, has proved to be a corruptive and unmanageable instrument for trying to accomplish the laudable goal of encouraging and assisting the upward mobility of those groups in

---

46 Lina A. Groglia, Southwestern University Law Review, Vol. 9, No. 3, 1977, pp. 593-594.

47 Richard Rodriguez, Politicks, December 6, 1977, pp. 13-14.

our society that have not made it into the economic mainstream. Well, what can we do to move toward that goal effectively? First, a concerted effort should be made to legislate the abolishment of the federal policy of compulsory affirmative action, and at the same time a major effort should be made to strengthen a federal policy of equal opportunities for qualified candidates. There should also be specific recommendations for alterative means which will be more effective in accomplishing the purposes originally proclaimed for affirmative action.

Before examining some suggestions as to what those alternatives might be, there needs to be consideration of three thorny theoretical dimensions of affirmative action. First, this policy, once established, initiates a vicious circle of fragmenting the populace into groups vying with each other to convince the authorities of their respective degree of disadvantage. As illustrated by Richard Rodriguez's essay, already white males in certain professions have moved into the category of seriously disadvantaged. Second, the use of underrepresentation of one or more groups in a given vocation is not a workable justification for affirmative action. If it were, then the colleges and universities have a lot of personnel changes to make in order to bring the representation of Republicans on the faculty up to their proportion of the citizens. Third, if equality of circumstance serves as a rationale for retaining affirmative action, is our government prepared to make permanent arrangements to equalize the living circumstances of the unemployed and the employed? And if so, who will do the work?

Richard Rodriguez's analysis points to the first step. "Though minority-group students and faculty members were now present at senior American colleges and universities, the majority of ghetto teen-agers never graduated from high schools to a hopeful future. An important signal of inequity—the absence of minorities from higher education—was removed before root problems were attacked . . . The illusion of progress improved the image of educational institutions. Government officials and academic administrators were able to evade the serious accusation that most nonwhite Americans could not pursue higher education."[48]

The most obvious root problem is the formal schooling received by the youngsters. In 1978, the Carter administration announced its

[48] Ibid. p. 14.

intention to allocate extra federal funds to support school programs in reading, writing and arithmetic. That makes sense except for the fact that if something is designated as a general-purpose school, the *first* allocation of its budget should be directed to these basic skills. To imply that this is something extra now being made available by the generosity of the federal government may be an accurate reflection of just how badly confused the nation's educational priorities are. If the electorate is genuinely committed to helping the children of impoverished families improve their lot, then the overwhelming priority must be to equip the students with those skills that are required for even minimal success as a citizen, and minimal success as a productive employee. Those basic skills include not only the "three R's" but also discipline. The revival of training in these matters would be designed to provide the youngster with an understanding that abiding by the rules is a fundamental necessity in a free society, and also to teach the child to accept without resentment the fact that there are certain obligations he must meet—both of these attitudes being essential to effective performance in any job. Furthermore, character education and citizenship education would help to reestablish the school as an orderly place of work, rather than a jungle where the young congregate to do their own thing, the latter condition too often foreclosing any useful learning in many inner-city schools and discouraging able people from entering or remaining in the teaching profession.

It is the time for wise and thoughtful people to cast aside the veil of doctrinaire commitment to unworkable policies and to labor responsibly, firmly and forthrightly to find better ways to meet the valid educational needs of our less fortunate citizens.[49]

DOLLARS, THRIFT, TIME, CONTENTION, ETC.

The techniques which the government has chosen for distributing federal funds to the schools and colleges are exceedingly costly. Not only must the government employ thousands and thousands of people to process, record and monitor the granting of funds to the schools and colleges of the country, but the recipient institutions have to employ their own

---

[49] Most of this analysis of affirmative action is drawn from a longer essay by the author in the booklet, Corporate Responsibility, Rockford College Institute, 1978, pp. 67-80.

thousands and thousands of people to process, record and monitor the grants back in the other direction. There is nothing productive or useful about all this processing. How much wiser it would be for impoverished educational institutions and impoverished national treasury if this processing could be reduced or even eliminated!

Another aspect of the existing system of federal funding is that there is little incentive for the grant recipients to economize. Since the funds allocated through many governmental programs are for specific purposes, the tendency is to use up the entire amount, even if that involves some peripheral or frivolous expenditures to do so. By contrast, funds that are available to an educational institution for whatever purposes it judges most important are subject to internal audits, economies and reallocations, according to the specific circumstances and changing priorities of that institution.

Apart from the costs of grant-processing and the disincentive for thrift, the federal government's role in education increasingly pre-empts administrative time, creates factions within the institution and distorts other aspects of the educational enterprise. Stanford University President Richard W. Lyman has written:

> ". . . it is undeniable that the regulatory climate for universities has changed remarkably in a short span of years, and that, in sum, the changes have produced enormous increases in our costs,[50] additions to our administrative staff, a boon to the paper industry of awesome proportions, and a source of friction and litigiousness which in itself constitutes a fairly heavy penalty for whatever improvements in our behavior as institutions the regulators have managed to generate. Seldom do university presidents congregate these days without their conversation turning to the latest skirmish with 'the Feds'—the very term suggesting a relationship of diminished cordiality between the universities and the national government."[51]

---

50 "In a single year, Harvard spent 60,000 man-hours complying with five federal regulations at a cost of $8.3 million." Jenkin Lloyd Jones, Wisconsin State Journal, April 15, 1979.

51 Bureaucrats and Brainpower, p. 30.

Although President Lyman chooses to summarize the academic-federal relationship in low-key terminology, the fact is that there is virtual unanimity in the academic community that the growing federal intervention in campus matters is a grave threat to the proper working of the university, and many share the view expressed by Harvard's President Bok last year that the most critical issue faced by his university is "its independence and freedom from ill-advised government restraint."[52]

POLITICIZATION

It has not been widely recognized that the massive federal funding of education has tended to make political captives of millions of our citizens. Particularly in this era when the population age spread of the nation indicates declining student enrollments, those people whose livelihood is dependent upon the educational system are *forced by pocketbook pressures* to favor whichever candidates for national office promise the highest level of federal subsidy for education. This group not only includes all the teachers, professors, librarians, administrators and maintenance personnel employed by the schools and colleges, and their families, but also the employees of a vast network of activities and professions whose livelihood is also dependent upon a prosperous educational system. Among the latter would be the publishers of textbooks and academic journals, the manufacturers of classroom furniture and laboratory equipment, firms which provide food services to schools and colleges, and many others.

The rising political militancy of the National Education Association, always in behalf of candidates which promise the most federal funding, is only the visible tip of the iceberg of a vast segment of the population caught in the trap of dependence upon this flow of federal funds.

Even more sobering, perhaps, than this large and increasingly organized political bloc is the question of how the built-in political captivity may skew the substance of what is taught in the classrooms. How objective can an individual be whose earnings will be affected by which party and which candidates win in the next election?[53]

---

52 Jenkin Lloyd Jones, Wisconsin State Journal, April 15, 1979.

53 [In 1972, the National Education Association, NEA, put heavy emphasis on the selection of Senator Clayborn Pell, the Federal Aid advocate who chaired the Senate Subcommittee on Education. After the election, Senator Pell said, "My

A WAY OUT OF THE TROUBLES

> "We should be apprehensive about a future in which all moral authority has been weakened, all institutions diminished in stature, and we are held together, tenuously at best, by thickening webs of regulation devised and enforced by growing bureaucracies."[54]

Mr. President, earlier generations of educational philosophers and college officials were fearful of the consequences of extensive federal subsidy of the educational system. The foregoing commentary on some of the more grievous educational problems caused or aggravated by the federal government indicates that our nation has made a mistake in failing to heed the judgment and the warnings of our predecessors.

We cannot undo that which has been done. Nor can we simply terminate the flow of Washington dollars without doing irreparable damage to our educational system which has many merits as well as unlimited potential to serve our nation well. Is there, then, some technique by which the government could disengage itself from the deleterious aspects of government funding and still make the requisite financial resources available to American education? I believe there is.

What is proposed is the utilization of a tax credit for contributions as the mechanism for transferring funds from federal resources to educational institutions, and it is suggested that it would be most easily tested at the college level. To illustrate the technique, suppose that a bill were enacted which granted the individual taxpayer a tax credit of $50 for his contributions to any college or university, public or private, that has been granted tax-exempt status by the federal government. Under this plan, the individual taxpayer may, if he wishes to do so, pay the first $50 of his tax bill to the college of his choice, and the rest of his tax obligation would be paid to the Internal Revenue Service.

---

election was a victory for teacher power. Before the teachers began to help me, I was a two-to-one underdog." Encouraged by their success in 1972, the NEA backed a presidential candidate in the next election and thereafter.]

54 Robert H. Bork. Convocation Address, Brigham Young University, 1979.

This proposal rests on several assumptions:

1. If the federal government is going to provide funds to support the educational function, it is best to do so in a manner which places the responsibility for deciding how these funds are spent in the hands of the people in charge of the educational program that spends them.
2. The intent is to find the most constructive system that is practicable for funding the educational process, and the fact that some citizens would be excluded from participation because their incomes are not large enough to pay $50 in taxes, while unfortunate, is not a proper cause for ruling out this plan from which they would benefit in other respects.
3. Since there must be some way of deciding who gets more and who gets less money, it is preferable to have those decisions made by neighbors, alumni and other individuals who are likely to know the most about the institutions receiving the money than to have a remote bureaucracy decide which institutions to support.
4. In the context of a government that is already extensively centralized, the tax credit is a valid and economical technique for encouraging the citizens to take certain actions judged beneficial to the national well-being.

The economies of this plan are substantial. It needs no expensive bureaucracies in Washington and regional offices to process any grants, nor the counterpart expensive bureaucracies on the campus to process them back again. The college receiving the taxpayer's gift simply sends him a receipt which he then affixes to his tax return as proof of payment of his first $50. Since the fund revenues from these tax credits would be at the disposal of the individual educational institution, its employees will benefit from every effort to spend each dollar with caution and thrift, thus protecting the economic viability of the employer.

The separation of church and state is in no way engaged in this method of funding. Gifts to churches and church-related educational institutions are already tax-exempt, so that to the extent the American taxpayers judge religiously based education important, that sector of education would prosper.

The small college would have a better chance to obtain its needed revenues under this system than it does in the present competition with the powerful university for Washington grants. Most of the alumni of the small college and many of its neighbors would be delighted to send it the first $50 of their tax obligations. Unless, of course, such people judged that a given college was not performing well and was unworthy of their help. The pressure under this system is for an educational institution to do a good job *educationally* in the eyes of those who know it best, in sharp contrast to the present system in which the college is judged according to whether it is delivering well on issues that were chosen because of *political pressures* on the government.

The colleges which serve black students and other minority groups would also benefit from this change. Currently, black institutions are in jeopardy under the interpretations of integration requirements. President Andrew Billingsley of Morgan State University is outspoken in his defense of Morgan State's remaining a predominantly black institution. "'We made a mistake with the public schools in 1954, and a lot of people are still making it with regard to higher education, letting the black institutions be destroyed . . . . If all the institutions are white, with blacks scattered through them—which is some people's idea of integration—then blacks have no anchor. That's the mistake we made in 1954.'"[55] This system would undoubtedly strengthen the remaining black institutions greatly. Indeed, it would generate a major impetus back toward a genuine variety in many other dimensions, too, among institutions of learning. As Paul Seabury has noted, the present system of federal funding and federal regulation is a "leveling" process. Its effect is "to gradually or even spasmodically obliterate the dynamic diversity of higher education in the United States."[56]

When this tax-credit proposal was actively supported in the early and mid-1960's, it was introduced several times in the Congress. That

---

55 "Bill Raspberry, " 'Black' Schools Aren't Segregated," Chicago Tribune, February 121, 1980.

56 Bureaucrats and Brainpower, p. 23.

it is neither liberal nor conservative, but simply common sense, was evident in the list of congressmen who supported it on one occasion when Congressman John B. Anderson sponsored the legislation. The list of co-sponsors ranged from Congressman John Ashbrook all the way across the spectrum to Father Robert Drinan.

IMPLEMENTATION

It is suggested that this technique of government funding for education be tried out on a modest basis. Perhaps a determination could be made of a number of existing federal programs of educational subsidy which are judged to be of only marginal usefulness. Those could be discontinued and the tax-credit ceiling set at a level which would divert tax revenues from the treasury to the colleges in the amount that had been spent on the discontinued programs. In this manner, there would be no negative impact on the already strained federal budget. If the system works reasonably well, then, year by year, other programs could be phased out and the tax-credit ceiling raised accordingly. In time, the authority for making educational decisions would be returned more and more to the responsible officers of the educational institutions who, in turn, would have pressure on them to provide an educational program that an increasing number of citizens would judge worthy of their tax-credit gifts.

If this plan proves to be effective, it could ultimately be adapted to the elementary and secondary schools of the country. There will be those who will recoil from tax-credit philanthropy on the grounds that if the government makes such a provision for the colleges and universities, what is to stop other kinds of institutions and services from demanding the same benefits? The answer to that reservation might be that if the technique is highly beneficial for education, nothing would or should stop people from requesting a comparable opportunity in other areas, provided that programs of tax credits would be authorized only in those cases where they would serve to phase out existing programs of direct federal subsidy.

IN CONCLUSION

The problems which beset American education are pervasive and have reached an intensity where remedial action is urgently needed.

Many of these problems have been brought about or rendered more acute by the intervention of the federal government. Because education serves such a critical role in preparing the citizens to carry their share of responsibility in a free society, a failure to diminish the burdens which the government now imposes on the educational community will make all the other problems you face, as our chief executive, more difficult to handle.

Early in the 20th Century, the rapidly growing cohort of socialist and Marxist professors was very effective in recruiting converts for their political systems. As Gordon Chalmers noted, "They were gifted in convincing students that evil, itself, extensive and malignant, does not exist. Walter Lippmann, the editor of The New Republic, and one of America's great literary statesmen summarized the tragic transformation of education in America. What follows are excerpts from that speech.

Keynote Address at the Annual Meeting of the American Association for The Advancement of Science on December 29, 1940 "The State of Education in This Troubled Age"

The thesis which I venture to submit is as follows:

That during the past forty or fifty years those who are responsible for education have progressively removed from the curriculum of studies the western culture which produced the modern democratic state;

That the schools and colleges have therefore been sending out into the world men who no longer understand the creative principle of the society in which they must live;

That deprived of their cultural tradition, the newly educated western men no longer possess the ideas the premises, the rationale, the values or the deposited wisdom which are the genius of western civilization;

That the prevailing education is destined, if it continues, to destroy western civilization, and is in fact destroying it; . . .

> The men who wrote the American Constitution and the Bill of Rights were educated in schools and colleges in which the classic works of their culture were the substance of the curriculum. That transmission was held to be the end and aim of education.
>
> Modern education, however, is based on a denial that it is necessary, or useful, or desirable to transmit from generation to generation the religious and classical culture of the western world. It abandons and neglects . . . the study of the whole classical heritage of the great works of great men; . . .
>
> There is no common faith, no common body of principle; no common body of knowledge, no common moral and intellectual discipline. Yet the graduates of these modern schools are expected to form a civilized community. They are expected to govern themselves. They are expected to have a social conscience . . . . When one realizes that they have no common culture, is it astounding that they have no purpose? . . . that they worship false gods? That in the fierce struggle for existence they are tearing western society to pieces?
>
> We insist that everyone must be educated, yet there is nothing in particular that an educated man must know.[57]

A solid generalist, Walter Lippmann, anticipated the tragic meltdown of America's rational, intelligent system of schooling which had served America so well. His speech was obviously intended to be a wake-up call, but had little impact on American educators.

We turn now to the one element of the radical changes of the sixties that was most effective in destabilizing and sometimes demolishing America's social institutions. That was the pestilence of marijuana use as a common-place feature of American life. And we will also consider the academic community's primary role in bringing about that state of affairs and the noxious impact which the people's shoulder-

---

[57] http://www.votd.com/lipp.htm

shrug reaction to mind-altering drugs had on many aspects of the American society. Prior to the 1961 uprising at the Berkeley campus, marijuana smoking was largely restricted to jazz musicians and the jet set. However, after revolutionaries urged student radicals to promote it among students it spread quickly from campus to campus across the country like a tsunami.

From 1971-1973, I was a member of the National Commission on Marijuana and Drug Abuse and have continued to follow developments in the on-going arguments for and against legalization. In 1996, National Review presented a symposium entitled "The Drug War Is Lost" with articles favoring some degree of legalization by authors, all of whose commentaries were lacking pertinent facts. In 2005, Stanford's Hoover Institution published Drug War Deadlock with paired pro and con articles about the issue of legalization. Not one of them touched on the massive research conducted during three decades in many countries about the exceedingly harmful physical and psychological consequences of using the different mind-altering drugs, including marijuana.

In 2008, I wrote an overview of the research and international conferences on drug use.

The following is an abbreviated version of that monograph.

LEGALIZED MARIJUANA: A PENDING DISASTER

by Dr. John A. Howard, Senior Fellow

at The Howard Center for Family, Religion & Society
Member of The National Commission on Marijuana and Drug Abuse (1971-73)

Introduction

"The War On Drugs Is Lost." was the theme of a twenty-four page symposium published in the 3/13/96 issue of National Review. The participants in the symposium were Baltimore's Mayor Kurt Schmoke, Ethan Nadelmann, the director of a drug policy research institute, a federal judge, a former police chief, a psychiatrist, a professor of law and, of course, William F. Buckley, Jr. In his introduction to the symposium, Buckley states that all panel members "agree on movement toward legalization, even though we may differ on just how far."

It is difficult for a person not well informed about drug issues to resist the persuasion of these seasoned and intelligent spokesmen from a variety of professions concerned with recreational drug use and the enforcement of drug laws.

However, it would be an exceedingly unwise and tragic mistake for the nation to move toward drug legalization on the basis of arguments like those presented in these essays. All seven of the participants make statements which are misleading or untrue, either because they are unaware of pertinent critical facts, or, perhaps, from a desire to leave those facts unmentioned.

William Buckley claims that nobody has ever been found dead of marijuana. As one physician has remarked, "Saying no one ever died from smoking marijuana is like saying no one ever died from smoking tobacco." The April 2003 issue of The Australian Family Association's newsletter[58] provides its current report on "cannabis-related deaths:" 184 in Australia, 664 in the United States in 1999 (reported by the Drug Abuse Warning Network) and six cannabis-related cardiovascular deaths in Norway.

Mayor Schmoke speaks of the U.S. prohibition of alcohol as a total failure. In fact, it wasn't. The 10/16/89 issue of The New York Times contains an article by Dr. Mark Moore, Professor of Criminal Justice at Harvard's Kennedy School of Government. The article was entitled, "Actually, Prohibition Was a Success." "Alcohol consumption," he wrote, "declined dramatically during prohibition. Cirrhosis death rates for men were 29.5 per hundred thousand in 1911, and 10.7 in 1929. Admissions to state mental hospitals for alcoholic psychosis declined from 10.1 per 100,000 in 1919 to 4.7 in 1928." Apart from whether Prohibition of alcohol was or was not a wise decision for the nation, a sneering reference to Prohibition is a quick way to avert any consideration of a ban on drug use.

Mayor Schmoke tells of a political opponent who advocated "zero tolerance" for the banned recreational drugs. "Zero tolerance" declared the Mayor, "is more of a slogan than a policy." Again, not true. A number of countries and the U.S. Navy have instituted zero tolerance policies with a high level of success.

Joseph McNamara, the police chief with a Harvard PhD., derides the Christian missionaries from China who were powerful lobbyists favoring the Harrison Act, which in 1914 became the first U.S. law to criminalize drug use. McNamara says the missionaries viewed the taking of psychoactive drugs as sinful. Whether they did or did not, what the police chief may not know is that those missionaries were keenly aware of the devastation inflicted on China by the British victory in the Opium War, forcing China to remove its ban on importing opium. It is estimated that ninety million Chinese became opium addicts after the ban was removed.

---

[58] Family Update, 582 Queensbury Street, North Melbourne, 3051 Australia

Federal judge Robert Sweet urges that the Congress "end the criminalization of marijuana which is now widely acknowledged to be without deleterious effect." There may be a wide acknowledgment of that supposition, but it is totally without factual foundation. In September of 1998, Current Concerns,[59] a periodical published in Zurich, Switzerland, printed a statement by Professor Henri Baylon, President of the French National Academy of Medicine. It includes excerpts from the general conclusions arrived at in the 1992 International Colloquium on Illegal Drugs co-sponsored by the National Academy of Medicine and the City of Paris. Among those conclusions: "The harmfulness of cannabis (marijuana) is very well documented today, experimentally and clinically. This drug damages the central nervous system, the lungs, the immunological resistance and the reproduction functions . . . It is absolutely essential to start an information and prevention campaign which takes into consideration the legal as well as the health risks of using cannabis."

Psychiatrist Dr. Thomas Szasz states, "the war on drugs is a mass movement characterized by the demonizing . . . of certain objects and persons ('drugs,' 'addicts,' and 'traffickers') as the incarnations of evil." What is there to say about a distinguished scholar engaged in counter-demonization?

In an echo of Mayor Schmoke's dismissal of a zero tolerance policy, Yale Professor Stephen Duke asserts, "The prohibitionists' scenarios have no basis either in our history or in other cultures." Ethan Nadelmann, a former Princeton professor who had left the campus to become the Director of the Lindesmith Center in New York City, states, "so far as I can ascertain, the societies that have proved most successful in minimizing drug-related harm aren't those that have sought to banish drugs, but those who have figured out how to control and manage drug use through community discipline." The "so far as I can ascertain" phrase could provide cover for the ignorance of Mayor Schmoke, a part-time activist in these matters, but this declaration from an academic who describes himself as "the Director of the country's leading policy reform organization" is quite simply unbelievable.

In 1954, Japan was faced with a serious problem of amphetamine abuse, with an estimated 2,000,000 people involved, a quarter of them

59 Current Concerns, P.O. Box 927, CH 8044 Zurich, Switzerland

injecting the drug intravenously. A law was passed imposing penalties of three to six months in jail for the use or possession and more severe penalties for the manufacture or sale of the drug. The law was rigorously enforced. In the first year, 55,600 people were arrested for drug offenses. Two years later only 271 arrests were made. The prohibitionist policy was a success.

Nadelmann also states "a basic truth about drugs and drug policy" namely that "Most people can use most drugs without doing much harm to themselves or anyone else." For him to engage in voicing such untruths is of critical importance because he is a key figure in the increasingly pervasive War Against The War On Drugs. This war is lavishly funded by billionaires George Soros and Peter Lewis (who, according to Time Magazine,[60] is "a regular pot user") and John Sperling, who Time Magazine reports has given $13 million to campaigns to liberalize state drug laws with 100% victories in the 17 ballot initiatives he backed.

The gathering momentum of the marijuana legalization juggernaut lends urgency to this effort to unveil the truth about the years of marijuana research conducted in many nations which consistently have discovered harmful consequences of smoking marijuana, as serious as those declared by the French National Academy of Medicine.

PERHAPS THE FINAL POINT TO BE MADE IN THIS PREFACE IS THE MOST TROUBLESOME OF ALL. REPORTS OF THIS RESEARCH AND OTHER CIRCUMSTANCES THAT ARGUE AGAINST THE USE OF MARIJUANA HAVE LARGELY BEEN WITHHELD FROM THE AMERICAN PEOPLE BY A NEWS MEDIA BLACKOUT. IN 1976, COLUMNIST ROSCOE DRUMMOND PUBLISHED AN ESSAY IN THE CHRISTIAN SCIENCE MONITOR ENTITLED "CONSPIRACY OF SILENCE ON MARIJUANA." HE BEGAN, "THERE IS WIDESPREAD IGNORANCE CONCERNING THE GRIEVOUS HARM WHICH MARIJUANA IS DOING TO YOUNG PEOPLE. THE CAUSE OF THAT IGNORANCE IS ALMOST UNBELIEVABLE IT IS SO PERNICIOUS. LEADING NEWSPAPERS, NETWORK MEDIA, AND MANY LEADERS OF SCIENCE, THEOLOGY AND EDUCATION ARE ACTIVELY CLOSING THE AVENUES

[60] Time, 4 November, 2002, p. 59

OF PUBLICITY BY SUPPRESSING THE EVIDENCE OF EXPERT FINDINGS."[61]

This blackout was dramatically evident for the first time in 1972. In 1971, the U.S. Congress established a National Commission on Marijuana and Drug Abuse. It was provided with a generous budget to conduct research, hold public hearings, travel to foreign countries to interview key figures in drug control and research, and make recommendations to the President and the Congress concerning drug policy.

During the first of two years, the Commission studied only marijuana. At that time the Commission judged that not enough research had been done to make flat judgments about the nature and extent of the harm marijuana might cause to the users, but what was known strongly suggested caution. The Commission's report urged the Government to discourage the use of the drug.[62]

At the press conference in The Capitol announcing the Commission's formal report, Governor Raymond Shafer of Pennsylvania, the Chairman of the Commission, opened the session by stating that the Commission's Report on Marijuana contained a number of recommendations. However, he said that the first recommendation urging the Government to discourage the use of marijuana was the most important one. The Commission's report was the lead story in the news nationally that evening and the next morning. Recommendation number one was not mentioned.

A year later, at the press conference for The Commission's report on other mind-altering drugs, Governor Shafer opened the meeting with an announcement that the Commission had reaffirmed its earlier report. He reminded the media that the recommendation to discourage the use of marijuana was the most important one and he urged the media to stress it in their commentaries about the second report. Once again, a national blackout.

What follows is an overview, starting in 1961, of the criminalization of marijuana, the research into the nature of the drug and the consequences of its use, and the ever-growing agitation to legalize it.

---

61 Roscoe Drummond, Christian Science Monitor, 29 December, 1976, p. 23

62 Marijuana: A Signal of Misunderstanding, p 134, U.S. Government Printing Office, March, 1972

Smoking Marijuana: Internationally Prohibited

On January 24, 1961, a Plenipotentiary Congress was convened at United Nations Headquarters, fulfilling a 1958 resolution of the UN Economic and Social Council. The purpose was to draft a treaty that would coordinate the efforts of the member nations to block the recreational use of narcotic drugs, and to limit the production of such drugs to amounts needed for medical and scientific purposes. After two months of deliberations, the delegates, representing seventy-three countries, produced an agreement entitled "Single Convention on Narcotic Drugs."[63]

The Preamble states in part:

> The Parties,
>
> Concerned with the health and welfare of mankind . . .
>
> Recognizing that addiction to narcotic drugs constitutes a serious evil for the individual and is fraught with social and economic danger to mankind . . .
>
> Considering that effective measures against abuse of narcotic drugs require co-ordinated universal action . . .
>
> Desiring to conclude a generally acceptable international convention replacing existing treaties on narcotic drugs, limiting such drugs to medical and scientific use, and providing for continuous international control for the achievement of such aims and objectives . . .

The text of the treaty was printed in Chinese, English, French, Russian and Spanish and sent to the member nations for their formal acceptance and involvement. The United States became a signatory in 1967. In 1972, the Convention was amended by a UN Protocol. The ultimate agreement contains fifty-one articles identifying opium, cocaine and cannabis (marijuana and hashish) as the drugs to be controlled and

---

[63] Single Convention on Narcotic Drugs 1961 as amended in 1972, United Nations, New York City

specifies the actions member nations must take to fulfill the ambitious purposes of The Convention. Most of the nations signed up. At that time, governments around the world agreed that the three designated categories of psychoactive drugs, used recreationally, were sufficiently harmful as to require concerted restrictive action.

The Alternative Press, Also Known As The Underground Press, Was a Powerfully Effective Medium Through which America's Youth were Recruited for Marijuana and Radicalism

The primary medium for spreading this infestation among the colleges was a phenomenon virtually unknown to the adults of that era, the alternative media. What follows is an extended quotation from the first chapter of the book bearing the title, The Alternative Media. The author, Francis M. Watson, Jr., had been an officer in the U.S. Army Intelligence and undertook to learn as much as he could about these publications and the actions they promoted. The quotation is incorporated here with his permission.

> The forebears of the alternative press were a small group of avant-garde publications that appeared in the mid-1950s, among them the *Village Voice* and the *Realist*, both of New York City, and the *Berkeley Barb*, Berkeley, California.
>
> The real surge of underground papers did not come until a decade after the *Village Voice* hit the streets of Greenwich Village in 1955. The "undergrounds" began to multiply when the fervor and experience generated in the civil rights movement were redirected to issues brought into prominence by Mario Savio and his cohorts in their confrontation with the University of California at Berkeley.
>
> Taking their cue from the printed materials that had proliferated in the metropolitan "hippie" communes, activist-prone college students, drop-outs and hangers-on began to produce their own tracts, pamphlets and tabloids designed for a campus clientele. The causes

were many: The ongoing concern for civil rights, sexual liberation, "filthy speech," agitation against the Vietnam War, psychedelic drugs, draft evasion, and the elimination of campus parietal rules constituted a heady brew, proclaimed with indignant self-righteousness under the banners of social justice and freedom. Other issues were soon added: the demand for student determination of the academic program, the insistence that military research not be tolerated in the academy, the call for the elimination of ROTC, the hue and cry against the military-industrial complex, and the barring of the campus to corporate and military recruiting officers.

As these cause-oriented papers broadened the range of issues to be covered and increased the intensity of their attacks on the institutions and practices of the society, they also broadened their audiences. They reached out into the high schools and penetrated military bases, both in the U.S. and overseas. There evolved an editorial amalgam of cultural rebellion and radical politics. The underground press was born—and it caught on. It spread from California and New York into other states on the West Coast and in New England, into the Midwest, down the East Coast, and into the South. The number of papers published throughout the country jumped from a mere handful in 1964 and 1965 to more than 800, in some 40 states, by late 1971.

They were hailed by their defenders, mainly in academia, as the "new journalism" or, even then, as "alternative papers," and sometimes as the "journalism of dissent." They were praised as outlets for the newly found "social awareness" of the youth.

This "awareness" soon turned to bitterness. Laurence Leamer, the young *Newsweek* writer who traveled about the country visiting with and interviewing members of the staffs of underground papers, wrote that when "they looked for new tools to end racism in America and bring the GIs home from Vietnam, they were drawn inexorably not toward a revitalized cultural radicalism but to Marxism and political revolution. These ideas could not help but affect the underground press, and by 1971 there were many papers that thought of themselves as propaganda weapons in the struggle for worldwide Marxist revolution."[64]

Many of these papers moved deeper and deeper into the politics of the far left, justifying this transition by claiming complete frustration in trying to "work within the system." Increasingly, they identified with Che Guevara, Castro, Mao Tse-tung, Lenin and Trotsky.

Although the name "underground" papers had been in use for some time, that designation took on a fuller meaning. Identifying themselves with the World War II underground papers in fighting against fascism and Nazism, a number of papers began to call America a "fascist state" and spelled it Ameri*k*a, sometimes working a swastika into the *k*. They proclaimed their kinship with modern rebels and revolutionaries around the globe—German and Italian terrorist groups, Irish rebels, Palestinians, various African organizations, "people's armies" in Argentina and Brazil, the Tupamaro guerrillas in Uruguay, and the National Liberation Front in Vietnam. They published countless suggestions about the tactics and weaponry for carrying out the "revolution" in the United States . . .

The main event was the undermining of the traditional institutions, values, relationships and patterns of conduct of the society.[65] The underground papers

---

64 Laurence Leamer, The Paper Revolutionaries, Simon and Schuster, New York, 1972, p. 83

65 The National President of Students for a Democratic Society (SDS), the most powerful group of radical students with a membership of 100,000, wrote in his book, The Sixties, Years of Hope, Days of Rage, (Bantam Books, 1987,) "By the late sixties, many of us had concluded the problem wasn't simply bad policy, but

> were kindling, stoking and fanning the fires of the counterculture. The government, the church, national foreign policy, the family, the educational system—all were castigated and ridiculed relentlessly.[66]

The Liberation News Service, the umbrella organization that served all the underground press, in 1969, stated, "The first thing drugs do is put you immediately outside the law. They give a lot of kids their first sense of belonging to a special group that's against the government."[67]

"What we are seeing is the artificial creation of a culture gap. A writer in the Ann Arbor Argus spoke of it as moving from a 'generation gap' to an 'interstellar war.' . . . [68] Other Scenes noted 'sex is one of the things that gets the other generation up tight . . . it's one of the things that revolutionaries use as an inexpensive, effortless tactic to upset people' . . . but in none of these is the society as likely to so strongly respond as drug usage."[69]

Even after all these years, very few people have any recognition how diabolical the marijuana stratagem was. In 1964, the United States was still basically an honorable and conscientious society that abided by the laws. To induce millions of students to adopt an illegal habit was a Marxist coup with repercussions far beyond the student body. With the parietal rules a thing of the past, many of the colleges, and ultimately almost all of the them, made no serious effort to prevent student use of the drug. Thus the colleges, by closing their eyes to this new pastime, became a party to harboring and covering up extensive and open defiance of the law. Thereafter colleges began to graduate generations with a casual or even disdainful attitude about lawfulness.

Both George Washington and Abraham Lincoln recognized the free society's absolute need for a lawful populace. In his Farewell Address,

---

a wrong-headed social system . . . alienation from American life—contempt, even, for the conventions of flag, home, religion, suburbs, shopping, plain homely Norman Rockwell order—had become a rock-bottom prerequisite for membership in the Movement core."

66 Francis M. Watson, Jr., The Alternative Media, Rockford College Institute, 1979, pp 3, 4, 5

67 Francis M. Watson, Jr., Tupart Review, Washington D.C., March, 1971, p. 6

68 Ibid., op. cit. p. 6

69 Ibid., op. cit. p. 6

Washington asserted "The very idea of the power and right of the people to establish government presupposes the duty of every individual to obey the established government. All obstructions to the execution of laws . . . are destructive of this fundamental principle and of fatal tendency." In his 1838 Lyceum Address, Lincoln expressed deep concern about "an increasing disregard for the law" and urged that reverence for the laws should become "the political religion of the nation."[70]

Additional dimensions of the induced alienation of the young people were: the Filthy Speech Movement; the fad of slovenly dress and grooming; a triumphant sexual experimentation and promiscuity; outrageous treatment of distinguished guest speakers, and the utilization of the mediums of bulletin boards, campus publications, football half-time shows, the classrooms and the campus theaters for language and subject matter previously ruled out by the traditional standards of piety, modesty, morality, decorum and civility. In addition to conning the college students into a nationwide habit of lawless conduct, the Marxists had also successfully savaged and virtually destroyed the civilized, cooperative and gracious environment of academia.

The magnitude of success in recruiting young marijuana smokers burst into the news in the summer of 1969. Four hundred thousand of them assembled in Woodstock, New York, for a rock music concert. The event was, in fact, also an insurrection, as the use of illegal drugs was unconcealed and pervasive. Within another year or two, the use of marijuana became a shoulder shrug for Americans, and not many years later, abiding by laws and rules and standards approached shoulder shrug status as well.

Three Decades of Research About the Consequences of Marijuana Use

The phenomenal sweep of marijuana use across the country and the 1969 Woodstock jamboree caused the United States Congress to enact the Comprehensive Drug Abuse Prevention and Control Act of 1970. That Act established the National Commission on Marijuana and Drug Abuse. Its bipartisan membership was comprised of two Senators, two

---

70 Schaub, Diana, "On the Character of Generation X," Public Interest, Fall, 1999, p. 22

members of Congress and nine members appointed by the President. Its tenure was two years with the first year restricted to a consideration of marijuana and the second a consideration of other mind-altering drugs including alcohol. The following are the provisions referring to marijuana:

> The commission shall conduct a study of marijuana including, but not limited to the following areas:
>
> (A) The extent of use of marijuana in the United States to include its various sources, the number of users, number of arrests, number of convictions, amount of marijuana seized, type of user, nature of use;
>
> (B) An evaluation of the efficacy of existing marijuana laws,
>
> (C) A study of the pharmacology of marijuana and its immediate and long term effects, both physiological and psychological,
>
> (D) The relationship of marijuana use to aggressive behavior and crime;
>
> (E) The relationship between marijuana and the use of other drugs, and
>
> (F) The international control of marijuana.

The published report after the end of the first year provided an insightful consideration of the cultural changes in America which disposed the young to use marijuana. Under the heading "Long-Term Effects" is a passage about social, psychological and behavioral changes "among the high school and college age Americans including many who have used marijuana heavily for a number of years. These changes are reflected by a loss of volitional goals. These individuals drop out and relinquish traditional adult goals and values. They become present rather than future oriented, appear alienated from broadly accepted social and occupational activity, and experience reduced concerns for personal hygiene and nutrition." The behavior described here, observed in numerous subsequent studies, became known as the amotivational syndrome.

The final passage in the Commission's marijuana report echoing the first recommendation, urged the Government to mobilize the voluntary sector of the nation to support the discouragement of marijuana use.

In 1974, two years later, the continuing rapid expansion of marijuana smokers led to a formal hearing before the subcommittee on Internal Security of the United States Senate Judiciary Committee. The hearings, entitled "Marijuana-Hashish Epidemic and Its Impact on United States Security, lasted from May 9th to June 13th and received testimony from many of the foremost marijuana research scholars of the world. Among them, senior professors from Oxford, the University of Paris, Cairo University, Berkeley, Columbia, the British Columbia Medical Association and the Karolinska Institute of Sweden.

The following statements are drawn from the introduction to the 430 page report of the hearings:[71]

> The testimony and documentations presented to the subcommittee . . . establish beyond any challenge that the epidemic was encouraged and facilitated by a widespread propaganda in favor of marijuana. It was recommended in glowing terms to the young people of our country.
>
> The epidemic spread of marijuana was also encouraged by the belief that it was a harmless as well as pleasant drug. The myth of harmlessness was based on no scientific evidence; actually, hard scientific evidence on the effects of chronic cannabis use has become available only in the last few years . . . .
>
> . . . The subcommittee arranged for the testimony of more than twenty top-ranking scientists, most of them medical researchers, some of them psychiatrists . . . . The collective testimony of the scientists . . . points to massive damage or potential damage to the entire cellular process, to the reproductive system, and to

---

71 Marijuana-Hashish Epidemic and Its Impact on United States Security, 1974 National Documentation Institute Summary Pamphlet P.O. Box 17121 Washington DC 20041

> the respiratory system. The evidence also points to the possibility of brain damage and genetic damage.
>
> Some of the scientists said that, on the basis of the information now available, they consider it the most dangerous drug with which we must contend today.

The collective testimony of the eminent scientists who came to Washington to testify may be summarized as follows:

1. THC, the principal psychoactive factor in cannabis, tends to accumulate in the brain and sex organs and other fatty-tissues. This was established beyond challenge by National Institute for Mental Health Nobel Laureate, Dr. Julius Axelrod . . .
2. Marijuana, even when used in moderate amounts, causes damage to the entire cellular process; it reduces DNA and RNA synthesis within the cell which sharply reduces the rate at which cells give birth to new cells. In the case of . . . the cells involved in the immune process, marijuana use at the three-times-a-week level results in a 41% reduction in cell birth. (Dr. Akira Morishima, Columbia University College of Physicians and Surgeons; Dr. Cecile Leuchtenberger, Head of the Department of Cell Chemistry, Institute for Experimental Cancer Research, Lausanne, Switzerland; Professor W.D.M. Paton, Head of the Department of Pharmacology, Oxford University; Dr. Gabriel Nahas, Research Professor at the Columbia University College of Physicians and Surgeons.)
3. . . . There is growing evidence that marijuana inflicts irreversible damage on the brain, including actual brain atrophy, when used in a chronic manner for several years. (Professor Robert Heath, Chairman of the Department of Psychiatry and Neurology at Tulane University Medical School; Dr. Harvey Powelson, Research Psychiatrist, University of California at Berkeley; Dr. Harold Kolansky,

Director of Child Psychiatry, Albert Einstein Medical Center, Philadelphia) . . .

5. Chronic cannabis smoking can produce sinusitis, pharyngitis, bronchitis, emphysema and other respiratory difficulties in a year or less, as opposed to ten to twenty years of cigarette smoking to produce comparable complications. (Dr. Forest Tennant, Jr. Officer in Charge of the Drug Abuse Program for the U.S. Army Europe, 1971-72; Dr. William T. Moore, Associate Professor of Clinical Psychiatry, University of Pennsylvania School of Medicine) . . .

7. Chronic cannabis use results in deterioration of mental functioning, pathological forms of thinking resembling paranoia and a "massive and chronic passivity" and lack of motivation, the so-called "amotivational syndrome." (Professor Nils Bejerot, Kolinska Institute Sweden, widely recognized as one of the foremost international experts in the field.)

In July of 1978, a Symposium on Marijuana was held in Reims, France, in conjunction with the Seventh International Conference of Pharmacology. A hundred senior scientists from fourteen nations took part. The research reported at the Symposium added new dimensions of information about the biological and medical harm which smoking marijuana does to the user of the drug. In the published papers of the Symposium, Oxford's Professor W.D.M. Paton provides the Concluding Summary. His text ends with the statement, "Cannabis satisfies the usual criteria for an addictive drug."[72]

In 1980, a major international symposium on "Drug Abuse, In The Modern World" took place at The College of Physicians and Surgeons of Columbia University. Forty-seven scholars, scientists, physicians, research specialists, clergy and educators presented papers. The organizers were Dr. Gabriel Najas, Dr. Henry Brill and The International Medical Council on Drug Use. For the book of the proceedings, published by

72 Copy of The Symposium Program

Pergamon Press, Jacques-Yves Cousteau provided a Preface. He wrote: "This book emphasizes the pharmacological effects of addictive drugs on their primary target, the brain. The human brain, by its very nature, especially in adolescence is most vulnerable to the drug-induced "high" and most tempted to recreate its effortless exhilaration."

In their Foreword, the editors wrote, "The purpose of this conference was to assess the impact of an unprecedented use of addictive drugs on man and society, especially in the United States where systematic studies and surveys of drug abuse in all its aspects are available . . . One message was clear: when addictive drugs are easily available, they will be abused on a large scale. Elsewhere in the volume, the editors noted, "This conference was ignored by the media. The term boycott cannot be used since two reporters showed up, one from the professional press, the other from a radio network. And yet about one hundred representatives of the local and national press (daily and weekly), Radio and T.V. had been informed several times of this conference."[73]

Brief excerpts from three of the presentations concerning marijuana.

> "Effect on Children and Adolescents of Mind-Altering Drugs With Special Reference to Cannabis" by Dr. Doris Milman, Professor of Pediatrics, State University of New York, Downstate Medical Center, Brooklyn

> . . . With cannabis usage among high school students rising from 45% in 1975 to 54% in 1979. With respect to age of initiation, 14% of children below the 9th grade were using marijuana in 1979 [statistics from US Department of Health, Education and Welfare.] . . .
>
> With more refined psychological investigative techniques, a myriad of cognitive and emotional changes have been defined. The most important cognitive effects are impairment of recent memory and retrieval, attentional deficits, difficulties in central

---

73 Drug Abuse In The Modern World Gabriel Nahas and Henry Clay Frick, II, eds Pergaman Press, New York, 1981 E. op. cit. p. 163

processing, altered time perception, visual distortions and hallucinations. Among emotional effects are mood fluctuations, including euphoria, listlessness, apathy and depression. Other emotional responses include drowsiness, indolence, withdrawal, anxiety and apprehension. Hallucinations, paranoid delusions, and feelings of depersonalization are not uncommon. [Dr. Milman's statement cites twenty-nine research reports from scholarly journals as the sources of this summary.][74]

"Hashish Use In Soviet Russia"
by Dr. Boris M. Segal, Chief of Substance Abuse Services at Montrose Veterans Administration Hospital

Five hundred high school students from Soviet Georgia who were heavy smokers were examined by the author. They displayed the following symptoms and emotional disorders. Euphoria followed by mild anxiety and depression, apathy, impairment of memory and thinking processes, loss of former friends and loss of interest in academic work, hostility toward parents, teachers and other authorities. At the beginning of smoking sexual activity increased and a proneness to promiscuity developed, but after a period of ingesting large doses, sexual interest decreased.

. . . The USSR is a party to the Single Convention of Narcotic Drugs and is intent on respecting its obligations under this treaty. There is no talk of "decriminalization" in Russia.

. . . The general consensus of Soviet Russian physicians is that hashish is dangerous to man and to society.[75]

---

[74] Ibid., op. cit. p. 48

[75] Ibid., op. cit. p. 247

"Drug Addiction: Relation to the Brain Mechanism for Reward and Implications for Survival" by Dr. Robert J. Heath, Department of Psychiatry and Neurology, Tulane University Medical School

> Objective studies have shown that profoundly destructive complications inevitably result from drug manipulation of the fundamental pleasure—pain mechanism . . . statements from our patients who were marijuana smokers that, in time, the pleasurable response to the drug was being attenuated and replaced by unpleasant feelings of oppression and paranoia.[76]

The research about marijuana and its use continued in many nations. Consumers' Research Magazine reported on the dangers of marijuana use in its March 31, 1980 issue, noting that more than 1,000 research projects had been completed on the drug.

Other notable conferences were the First International Symposium on the Physiopathology of Illicit Drugs held in Paris on May 31, 1990. Among other findings, it was reported there that of 204 case-control pairs of mothers, the ones who were marijuana-users prior to, or during pregnancy had an eleven-fold increased risk of having babies who developed nonlymphocytic leukemia.[77]

The Second International Symposium Against Drugs in Switzerland took place April 12 and 13, 1997, in Stadtsaal Zofingen. The International Organizing Committee was comprised of sixteen Physicians, Scholars and Drug Abuse professionals from Canada, France, Italy, Netherlands, Sweden, USA and Switzerland. The program noted, "In advance of the Swiss referendum on "Youth Without Drugs" which will be held later this year, the 2nd Symposium is intended to provide information and to stimulate thinking which will be valuable in the development of an informed public opinion. [The underlining has been added.][78]

---

76 Ibid., pp. 3, 4

77 Report on the Symposium, Reproductive Toxicology, Vol. 5, pp 389-90, 1991

78 Program of the Symposium

Another drug symposium worthy of mention is the one held in Wellington, Kansas (pop. 8400) on February 20 and 21, 1980. A local physician, Dr. Eugene C. McCormick, had attended the Second Annual Symposium on Marijuana held at New York University Post-Graduate Medical School in 1979. He was determined to have his community informed about marijuana. A widely publicized two-day program featuring noted speakers attracted an attendance of more than 3,000 people!! Americans want to be informed by the experts on this subject.[79]

On September 18, 2002, The New York Times printed as a full-page ad, An Open Letter To Parents About Marijuana. The text begins:

> Marijuana puts kids at risk. It is the most widely used illicit drug among youth today and is more potent than ever. Marijuana use can lead to a host of significant health, social, learning, and behavioral problems at a crucial time in a young person's development . . . And don't be fooled by popular beliefs. Kids can get hooked on pot. Research shows that marijuana can lead to addiction. More teens enter treatment for marijuana abuse each year than for all other illicit drugs combined.

The ad is signed by eighteen organizations. Among them are American Academy of Family Physicians, American Academy of Pediatrics, American College of Emergency Physicians, American Medical Association, American Society of Addiction Medicine, Child Welfare League of America, National Center for School Health Nursing, National Medical Association and the National Parent Teachers Association.

The Children's Drug Culture

The feature article of The New York Times Sunday Magazine of 2/10/80 was entitled "New Parental Push Against Marijuana." The subtitle was

[79] Citizens for Informed Choices on Marijuana Newsletter Vol. II, No. 1 300 Broad Street, Stamford CT 06901

"A dramatic increase in the use of pot by teen-agers and young children has parents all over the country revving up for the anti-drug battle." The following are highlights of the article.

> During the last two years, hundreds of antipot parents' organizations have sprung up, unheralded, around the nation . . . . Their children are part of a new generation of young pot smokers who start at an earlier age, smoke grass more than 10 times as strong [as the 1960s] and light up before, after and during school hours . . .
>
> The dean of students at the high school in Greenwich, Connecticut, reports that pot-smoking, 'starting in the lower grades' has become an integral part of growing up and often reaches the level of heavy dependence by junior high school. The publisher of <u>Accessories Digest</u> [pot-smoking accessories] even acknowledges that the early use by children results in "wasted kids, a sad situation" . . .
>
> The president of the largest private drug-treatment program, Phoenix House, notes that if young people take up marijuana early, "they establish a pattern of escaping rather than dealing with reality. They do not learn how to cope" . . .
>
> One woman tells of her 12-year-old-daughter who had turned into "a sullen, alienated, unreasonable creature." Dr. Harold Voth of the Menninger Clinic stated that marijuana is the great alienator.

The article tells of people in Essex County, New Jersey, whose appeal to the local Bureau of Narcotics resulted in convening a special grand jury. The grand jury report stated, "Marijuana use among our young may be the most dangerous situation we have faced as a nation in many years." The use of pot in the schools even involved 8-year-olds who were smoking and dealing. The use of the drug was "open, notorious and pervasive."

Is it any wonder that the 1986 Pamphlet of the U.S. Department of Education, "Schools Without Drugs," stated that marijuana-using students were twice as likely as other classmates to average D's and F's in their schoolwork and twice as likely to drop out of school?

Impaired Functioning of Marijuana Users

In 2002, the Robert Wood Johnson Foundation and the National Highway Traffic Commission reported on their national study of automobile drivers who were under the influence of illegal drugs.[80] They estimated there were nine million such drivers and called upon the states to adopt criminal laws setting strict standards against the presence of illegal drugs in the driver's body "Driving under the influence of drugs is a growing national problem, particularly among young people, but drugged drivers are not detected nearly as often as drunk drivers" according to the report. In its article "How Safe Is Pot?" Newsweek (1/7/89) noted, "Most investigators now agree that marijuana does share with alcohol the danger of impairing coordination and judgment among its users."

Dr. Gabriel Nahas has repeatedly reported on the danger of driving while high on marijuana. "Although alcohol tends to make drivers more aggressive, marijuana has much stronger effects on the estimation of time and distance. This affects the accurate estimation of how much time is needed to overtake when passing another car . . . . [with marijuana] there is still a marked deterioration of driving skills 5 to 6 hours after intake and some subjects, 8 to 10 hours after intake . . . Thus the driver may still be influenced when he believes he is no longer "high."[81]

"A six month sampling of persons stopped for erratic driving by the California Highway Patrol discovered that roughly one in four showed blood samples containing tetrohydracanabinol, the active ingredient in marijuana.[82]

"A sky-diving instructor who died in July while attempting to land on a pond . . . was seriously impaired by smoking marijuana within two hours of his death according to a toxicology report."[83]

---

80 "Many, Undetected, Use Drugs and Then Drive" New York Times, 15 November, 2002

81 Gabriel Najas, Keep Off The Grass Pergamon Press, New York, pp. 107, 8

82 "Marijuana Smoking in Public Increases as Penalties Drop," New York Times 28 November, 1977

83 "Skydiver smoked marijuana before fall" Chicago Tribune 12 September, 2002

"Investigators are still trying to determine if the motorman responsible for the crash of a Chicago elevated train on February 4—killing 11 persons and injuring 160—was using pot at the time. While the motorman denies it, officials found a case containing four marijuana cigarettes, traced to him in the rubble."[84]

"A federal appeals court set aside an Arizona Death Row inmate's sentence ruling that the condemned murderer is entitled to hearings on whether the marijuana addiction of the judge who oversaw his trial tainted the outcome."[85]

The business community pays a high price for the marijuana-impaired performance of employees. According to The Journal of the American Medical Association Marijuana users had 55% more industrial accidents, 85% more injuries and had an absenteeism rate 78% higher than non-drug-users.[86]

Another aspect of collateral harm from marijuana smoking is cited by Dr. David Powelson, Chief of Psychiatry at Cowell Hospital at the University of California. He "made this comment in 1967, 'Marijuana is harmless. There is no evidence that it does anything but make people feel good . . . . It should be legalized.' Eleven years later, after having examined thousands of students who have used marijuana, Dr. Powelson has stated, 'I now believe that marijuana is the most dangerous drug we must contend with.' He gives three reasons: . . . 1) early marijuana use is beguiling and the user cannot detect any mental deterioration; 2) continued use of marijuana leads to such deterioration; 3) the users of marijuana display a strong need to seduce others into using the drug.'"[87] Neither cigarette smokers nor users of alcohol feel compelled to convince others to join in their indulgence, but this need to bring in one's acquaintances and associates is a recurrent observation among marijuana analysts. Indeed in 1972, the Report of The National Commission on Marijuana stated, "Most of the Americans who have used marijuana have been merely experimenting with it . . . About 2%, or 500,000 people, now use the drug heavily . . . The heavy marijuana

84 The Mindzenty Report, March 1977

85 "Execution ordered by addiction judge is off," Chicago Sun Times 14 October, 2001

86 Journal of the American Medical Association, vol. 264, pp. 2639-2643, 1990

87 David Asman "Has Princeton Turned To Booze," Prospect Summer, 1978 p. 12

user presents the greatest risk to health. It is the Commission's opinion that these heavy users constitute a source of contagion within American society. They actively proselytize others into a drug oriented life."[88] As in any plague, the people afflicted with this malady contaminate others.

The Campaign To Legalize Recreational Drug Use

The organized effort to legalize marijuana was begun in 1971 by Keith Stroup, a young lawyer who had served in the Federal Government. The name he chose for the new organization was originally The National Organization for the Repeal of Marijuana Laws, leading to the clever acronym, NORML. The former U.S. Attorney General, Ramsey Clark, convinced Stroup to change the word "Repeal" to "Reform," a term much more palatable to the general public. Clark became a member of his National Board of Advisors, as did Hugh Hefner, Geraldo Rivera, Benjamin Spock, Congressman Ron Dellums, Senator Jacob Javits and other notables including several Harvard Professors. The Playboy Foundation provided $15,000 of seed money and afterwards made very generous annual grants.

A year after NORML was activated, the Drug Abuse Council was created by the Ford Foundation to determine how private foundations might be helpful in addressing the drug problem. The two Washington lawyers hired to do a preliminary study decided that recreational drugs were a given of human existence so that the need was to educate the populace how to use them properly. "An approach emphasizing suppression of all drugs or repression of drug users," they wrote in a report to the Ford people, "will only contribute to national problems."

The Drug Abuse Council and NORML were instant compatriots. The Council was launched with ten million dollars of grants from the Ford, Carnegie, Kaiser and Commonwealth Foundations, and a star-studded Board of Directors from business, law and academia. Among other early donors were the United Methodist Church and the U.S. State Department. Dr. Thomas Bryant, was named President of the Council, who, like the Directors, had no professional expertise or experience in drug dependence. Dr. Bryant became a member of NORML's Advisory Board and arranged for a monthly stipend for

88 National Commission on Marijuana and Drug Abuse, op. cit. pp. 81, 2

Keith Stroup as a consultant to the council. Dr. Bryant assembled a staff of academics trained in law, sociology, journalism and political science. None of them was knowledgeable in any of the fields related to the nature of the drug and the consequences of using it. The council concluded its work and submitted a final report in 1980 endorsing decriminalization of the drugs.

The alliance with The Drug Abuse Council was very beneficial to NORML. The Council provided NORML with instant prestige and credibility and access to the eminent scientists and policy-makers who became involved in the Council's work.[89] NORML grew rapidly, establishing chapters in cities across the country and enlisting earnestly partisan members.

At NORML's sixth annual meeting in 1977, the sessions dealt with the standard fare of such gatherings—the alleged relative harmlessness of the drug, the civil rights of drug users, "horror" stories of mistreatment by police and the courts, therapeutic benefits that have been identified for glaucoma and pain relief among certain cancer patients—but the overriding theme of the membership was, "We like to smoke pot and we don't want to be arrested for it." (Many did smoke pot during the meetings, even in the presence of speakers and panelists who were federal officials, and were not arrested.)

Emotionalism, shallow reasoning and a flat assumption that marijuana laws are to be ignored characterized much of the commentary from the floor as well as some of the platform presentations. Insults and obscenities greeted any speaker who dared to disagree with the pro-marijuana thrust, and one such speaker was assaulted with a pie. In that particular session, an officer of the government spoke of the international barriers to legalization. The point was greeted with vocal displeasure from the audience, the gist of which was, "Who cares about international treaties? We want to have the right to smoke pot."

In a statement to the conference, Director Stroup left no doubt that decriminalization is but a way station to larger objectives. "It does cause me some pause when the President of the United States now has the same official position towards marijuana that we do. It kind of says something to me. Number one, I'm glad to have his support, but

89 This information about The Drug Abuse Council is taken from Gabriel Nahas Cocaine: The Great White Plague, Eriksson Publisher, Middlebury, VT, 1089, pp. 106-8.

number two, I think it is about time we began to get out a little further ahead, and begin to point the direction for where we should be headed." This comment was greeted with shouts of approval.[90]

The Washington Post (4/10/78), reported that NORML's next annual conference was held at the Hyatt Regency Hotel with about 400 guests including White House staff members, other government representatives and various celebrities. The article told of Stroup's explaining why he smokes. "As usual, he appears confident to the point of arrogance. 'The reason most people smoke, and I'm really no different, is out of relaxation and fun. It's a recreational drug, a social lubricant. The most natural thing in my life is to light up a joint and pass it around. It's like 'Have a drink of my scotch and I'll have a drink of yours.'"

The chapters of NORML, guided and supported by the National Office, were very effective in their legislative initiatives. Decriminalization laws were passed in eight states by February, 1977. Playboy interviewed Stroup that month. "I think all drug use should be decriminalized," said he, "I've tried just about every drug except heroin . . . drugs can take you out of your hectic, trivial life and into a cosmic level."[91]

NORML sponsored a full-page ad in the 4/9/02 issue of the New York Times, featuring a very large photograph of New York Mayor Michael Bloomberg saying, "You bet I did, and I enjoyed it." This was his response to a question about marijuana use. The simple message of the ad is that if people enjoy doing something, they should not be prevented from doing it.

The concept that people should not be prevented by law from doing what they please as long as it harms nobody else is a foundational principle of libertarianism. A number of libertarian organizations and individuals have become active in the thrust to legalize recreational drugs in support of that principle regardless of whether they do or don't favor such drug use.

Milton Friedman, one of the world's foremost free market economists, has been a strong legalization advocate for many years. That the capitalistic system requires a minimum of governmental interference in order to prosper is an established fact. Whether that cardinal principle

---

[90] This information was provided by Francis M. Watson, Jr., who attended the meeting.

[91] Mindzenty Report, op. cit. p. 2

of economics is equally applicable to the successful operation of the non-economic dimensions of a society is open to question.

Humanity's progression from raw and brutal savagery to civilization cannot take place except as the people learn to subordinate their desires when that is required to serve the common good. Throughout life every person is subject to a running conflict between what he would like to do at a given moment and what he is called upon to do as a member of a family, a kindergarten, a work place, a citizen or a nation. In a smoothly operating free society, the citizens voluntarily abide by the standards and rules and laws which ideals and experience have caused to be established. A strong and viable free society is one in which self-subordination and self-discipline, without resentment, are prominent and necessary characteristics of the populace. In the present era wherein the assertion and institutionalization of innumerable rights have all but driven from the premises the behavioral obligations which once made America a civil and amicable society, the question is what other option than enforced laws can protect the children and youth from the pervasive, persuasive and predatory pro-drug advocates of the drug culture?

Both the CATO Institute and Reason Magazine provide intelligent and influential voices in behalf of libertarianism and both are engaged in the drug legalization effort. The January, 1978 issue of Reason Magazine published a five-page report entitled "Rockefeller's Draconian Drug Law." The article resulted from a study conducted under a grant from The CATO Institute and the Sabre Foundation.

A relatively recent entry into the battle for legalization is George Soros, financially, the eight hundred pound gorilla that has pre-empted center stage.

George Soros, Resolute Financier of Liberalized Drug Laws

The fortune of George Soros was set by the 2002 Forbes magazine rating at 6.9-billion dollars. He is generous with his money. Since 1982, he is said to have donated 3.8-billion dollars through his foundations in twenty-four nations.[92] When he backs a cause, he does so with the intention of accomplishing his purpose.

---

92 Adrian Karatnysky, "Messianic Billionaire," Philanthropy, Sept./Oct., 2002, p. 30

His first foundation was established in Hungary, his native land. The Soros activities in opposition to the Communist regime are said to have had a substantial part in bringing about the collapse of that regime.[93] In 2000, George Soros became acquainted with Alejandro Toledo, the leader of a group seeking to depose Peru's despotic Alberto Fujimori. Soon thereafter Toledo received a Soros gift of a million dollars that proved to be critical in toppling the Fujimori government, opening the door to Toledo's being elected Peruvian president. Soros also was extensively involved in the "Rose Revolution" which put an end to the regime of the allegedly corrupt government of Eduard Sheverdnadze in Georgia.[94]

The influence he exerts worldwide was summed up by Morton Abramowitz, former U.S. Ambassador to Turkey and now President of the Carnegie Endowment for International Peace. "Soros," he said, "is untrained, idiosyncratic, he gets in there and does it, and he has no patience with government. As I frequently say about George, he's the only man in the U.S. who has his own foreign policy—and can implement it."[95]

This worldwide mover and shaker was born in Budapest in 1930, when Hungary was plagued by Nazi occupation. As Jews, he and his family had to engage in constant subterfuge to avoid arrest, incarceration, deportation, and other brutalities inflicted on the Jews. That tense and fearful period, which he identifies as critically formative for him, seems to have scarred him with a stunted sense of compassion and human warmth. He was able to go to London in 1947 and earned a degree at the London School of Economics. Nine years later he moved to New York City and eventually became an American citizen. He had a meteorically successful career in hedge funds and international finance and in 1973, with a partner formed his own firm, The Quantum Fund. His Quantum Fund stunned the financial world when it successfully gambled fifteen billion dollars that the British pound would decline in value. And it did, and Soros became enormously wealthy and earned the title, "the man who broke the bank of England."

---

93 Ibid.

94 David Greising, "The New Face of Money in U.S. Politics," Chicago Tribune, 7/25/04

95 Connie Bruck, "The World According to Soros," The New Yorker, 1/23/95, p. 57

At the London School of Economics, he became engrossed in the philosophy of one of his professors, Sir Karl Popper. Popper's major work, The Open Society and Its Enemies, provided the central concept for the work of his foundations, many of them appropriately named Open Society Institutes. An "open society" is one in which the government does nothing to regulate the private behavior of the individual, providing he harms no one else. The Open Society, is, of course, the antithesis of Communism, but Soros perceives the American free society also to be an enemy of the Open Society as it involves itself in such matters as abortion, reproductive health, sexual behavior, sterile needle distribution, euthanasia, and the use of recreational drugs. Much of the recent anti-terrorism legislation is also abhorrent to George Soros, perceived as infringements on civil rights. For him, George Bush is the champion of a number of policies in sharp conflict with the principles of the Open Society, hence the enormous Soros financial investment in the anti-Bush election campaign.

In 1994, George Soros funded the establishment of the Lindesmith Center, in New York City, a think-tank devoted to the legalization of marijuana, launching it with a pledge of $4,000,000. It is named for the late Alfred Lindesmith, a sociology professor at Indiana University. He believed regulation was a far better way than prohibition and punishment to control recreational drugs. "The foundation for Lindesmith's social policy regarding drug addiction was the liberal philosophy of John Stuart Mill as expressed in his famous essay, On Liberty: 'Over himself, over his own body and mind, the individual is sovereign. In the part which concerns himself, his independence is of right absolute.' "[96] Lindesmith and John Stuart Mill were a perfect match for the "Open Society," especially that final, "absolute." Soros chose Ethan Nadelmann, a Princeton professor, to head the Lindesmith Center. Nadelmann, a well-known critic of U.S. Drug Policy, developed for the Center a full program of publications, public lectures, conferences, and writing Letters to the Editor, and articles for periodicals and newspapers. In 2000, the Lindesmith Center was merged with Soros's Drug Policy Foundation, a membership organization, to become the Drug Policy

---

[96] Gabriel Nahas, The Great White Plague, Eriksson, Middlebury, 1989, p. 85

Alliance, headed by Nadelmann. The Alliance is centered in New York City and has seven offices throughout the country.[97]

Ethan Nadelmann, George Soros' Guileful Ideological Warrior

Below is the statement on the Drug Policy Alliance's website (11/12/2004) about Ethan Nadelmann.

> Ethan Nadelmann, Executive Director
>
> Ethan Nadelmann is the founder and executive director of the Drug Policy Alliance, the leading organization in the United States promoting alternatives to the war on drugs.
>
> Nadelmann was born in New York City and received his BA, JD, and PhD from Harvard, and a Masters degree in International Relations from The London School of Economics. He then taught politics and public affairs at Princeton University from 1987 to 1994, where his speaking and writings in publications from Science and Foreign Affairs to American Heritage and National Review attracted international attention. He also authored the book, Cops Across Borders, the first scholarly study of the internationalization of U.S. criminal law enforcement.
>
> In 1994, Nadelmann founded the Lindesmith Center, a drug policy institute created with the philanthropic support of George Soros. In 2000, the growing center merged with another organization to form The Drug Policy Alliance which advocates for drug policies grounded in science, compassion, health and human rights. Described by Rolling Stone as "the point man" for drug policy reform efforts, Ethan Nadelmann

[97] Information drawn from Neil Hrab "George Soros' Social Agenda for America," Foundation Watch of the capital Research Center, April, 2003

> is widely regarded as the outstanding proponent of drug policy reform in the United States and abroad.

The purpose for which Keith Stroup founded NORML was unapologetically clear in the name he originally chose for NORML, The National Organization for the Repeal of Marijuana Laws. Stroup and his associates wanted to enjoy their pot-smoking legally.

In sharp contrast, George Soros, in taking up the matter of laws governing recreational drugs, was simply adding a dimension to his efforts in behalf of Karl Popper's open society. The protection of the principle of the individual's sovereignty over his person and his behavior seems to have been his compelling motive. Ethan Nadelmann, in his involvement with matters of drug policy has been similarly inspired by Alfred Lindesmith's aversion to governmental regulation. Nadelmann has found that this one-dimensional cause can be powerfully advanced by employing the techniques Marcuse and others prescribed to the student radicals.

In their plans for subverting the free society, beyond the alienation and radicalization of the youth, the Marxist mentors wished to corrupt and nullify the rational means by which the effective free society evaluates and adjudicates controversial matters.

Montesquieu dealt with the virtual impossibility of a free society's negotiating effective international agreements with a tyranny. The following quotation occurs in Book Four of The Spirit of Laws under the sub-heading, "That Honor is not the Principle of Despotic Governments."

> As honor has its laws and rules . . . it can be found only in countries in which the constitution is fixed and where [the nations] are governed by settled laws . . .
>
> Honor is a thing unknown in arbitrary governments, some of which have not even a proper word to express it.

When a Western nation signs a treaty, it expects to honor the treaty. But what about the despotism where honor has no meaning? Once this fixed and non-negotiable impasse is understood, it becomes possible to realize that the Soviet Communists' definition of truth as whatever advances their Marxist cause was not a joke, but a central operating principle of the system. After this astonishing concept sinks in, it becomes clear why the university officials who, in the 1960's were imbued with truthfulness and lawfulness, were stunned and confused and immobilized by the revolutionary activism of the Student Protest Movement.

Among the techniques urged upon the students for sabotaging the free society's system for addressing conflict with civility were:

1. Hijack the vocabulary of ideals, virtues and worthy goals and insist that these are the very attributes of your activity.
2. Assert brazen, discrediting lies about the goals, attributes and accomplishments of your adversaries.
3. Assert brazen, favorable lies about your own goals, actions, and accomplishments as publicly, forcefully and frequently as possible.
4. In public debate, determine what is the outermost leftist position and plant your banner far beyond that leftermost position and do so loudly and with deep conviction. [An extremely successful illustration of this technique took place when a professor at Rutgers publicly asserted his hope that the Viet Cong would win. This view was immediately trumpeted by student radicals across the country, and soon the immediate withdrawal of all troops which had previously been the extreme left position was converted to the moderate position.
5. Use these tactics to mobilize public fear of your adversary and anger at and contempt for your adversary and keep adding fuel to these public passions.
6. The end goal is to divide the nation into two groups: the good guys who are openly and enthusiastically on your side; and the bad guys.

Consider now, the data sheet published by the Drug Policy Alliance about its Executive Director, Ethan Nadelmann. The Alliance "advocates for drug policies grounded in science, compassion, health and human rights." As Hitler wrote in Mein Kampf, "Any lie will be believed if it is big enough." To assert that the policies advocated by the Drug Policy Alliance are grounded in science and health is breath-taking in its audacity. And compassion? Any activity that makes marijuana more readily available to eight-and nine-year-olds by liberalizing drug laws scarcely rates the designation of compassion.

"An End To Marijuana Prohibition: The drive to legalize picks up" is the title of a Nadelmann article in National Review 7/12/04. "No drug is perfectly safe," he writes, "and every psychoactive drug can be used in ways that are problematic." Problematic? To disguise the meaning of "toxic" by applying a label of "questionable" or "puzzling" is a dextrous device of idealogical warfare. He finds it necessary to use "problematic" again later in the article. In the same paragraph he writes, "The federal government has spent billions of dollars on advertisements and programs that preach the dangers of marijuana . . . But the government has yet to repudiate the 1988 finding of the Drug Enforcement Administration's own administrative law judge, who concluded after extensive testimony that "marijuana in its natural form is one of the safest therapeutically active substances known to man." Perhaps Nadelmann supposes his readers are too stupid to notice that his curt dismissal of the Government's reports of the various dimensions of harm caused by marijuana is tightly restricted to medical uses of marijuana. By introducing an irrelevant quotation from a governmental official he apparently hopes to have refuted the government's far-ranging warnings, a tricky ploy for diverting attention from a truth.

National Review provided an opportunity for John Walters, the director of the Office of National Drug Control Policy, to respond to Nadelmann's "End to Prohibition" Article. Walters provided an intelligent, forceful, but civil rebuttal in the 9/27/74 issue. Also in the issue is Nadelmann's response to Walters. Nadelmann begins his article: "I am grateful for John Walters's ill-considered rejoinder to my article, mostly because it demonstrates so well the disregard for science, lack of intellectual rigor, and passion for partisan insult that characterize the drug czar and his failure of a drug control policy." Later on he writes, "With respect to the broader issue of marijuana policy, Walters's broadside essentially amounts to a hodgepodge of mistakes, distortion and crude attacks. He ignores overwhelming evidence that most people who smoke marijuana do no harm to their health." This is pure Marxist dialectics, loudly and aggressively accusing the adversary of the short-comings of your own performance. The "do no harm to your health" is, as they say, "problematic."

A New York Times (10/10/99) article, by Nadelmann bears the title, "New approach to drugs that's grounded not in ignorance or fear, but common sense." Nadelmann begins by recommending, "Drop the 'zero-tolerance' rhetoric and policies and the illusory goal of a drug-free society. Accept that drug use is here to stay and that we have no choice but to learn to live with drugs." What he espouses is totally dependent upon sustaining the blanket of public ignorance about the success stories of zero-tolerance policies and about the wide range of physical and psychological harm caused by marijuana use, thoroughly documented by research scholars around the globe. He concludes the essay with, "What we're talking about is a new approach grounded . . . in common sense, public health and "human rights." Common sense? Public health?

The drug-legalizers do not address the arguments and data of the opposition, they simply deny them or ignore them. They seem incapable of pity or compassion for the thousands of young people living the half-lives of amotivational syndrome or for any of the other victims of marijuana use.

No-Tolerance Policies Do Work

As noted in the introduction, Yale Professor Stephen Duke said, "The prohibitionist's scenarios have no basis either in our history or other cultures." Several other participants in that symposium also scorned the concept of policies of interdiction. This notion is a standard argument in the rhetoric of drug legalizers. They are simply wrong, whether by ignorance, or deceit.

Japan was able not only to put an end to the widespread amphetamine addiction in 1954, but in the 1960's it also terminated a heroin problem which had involved more than 50,000 addicts. In both instances, a heavy penalty for possession or use was the means to success. In this modern industrial nation, the no-tolerance policy worked.

In the barely developing China of a century ago almost a third of the population was addicted to opium. The following description is drawn from an essay by Gabriel Nahas, "Drugs, The Brain and The Law."

> At the end of the 19th century, out of a population of 300 million, 90 million were addicted to opium . . . During the first part of the 20th century, a national revival stressing the basic values prevailed in the country and restored China 50 years later to the rank of a world power . . . It was a period of revolution and civil strife, putting traditionalists against reformers, nationalists against communists. But in spite of their conflicting allegiances, all of the Chinese were united in their determination to stamp out opium addiction.[98]

Not only was mainline China cleared of this plague, but so also were Taiwan and Singapore. In the summer, 1977, issue of NORML's periodical was a report of laws prohibiting marijuana possession. For South Korea, 7 to 10 years of hard labor; For Turkey, 3-5 years in jail strictly enforced; For Bolivia, 2-8 years in jail strictly enforced; For Syria, 6 months to life in jail, strictly enforced.

In the United States, by 1914 there were hundreds of thousands of Americans who had become addicted to patent medicines laced with cocaine. Many sanitariums were built to house the addicts. Under the leadership of President Theodore Roosevelt, the Pure Food and Drug Act was enacted in 1906. And in 1914 The Harrison Act was passed to restrict the non-medical use of cocaine and opiates. In ten years, the number of cocaine addicts was reduced by 80%. "This dramatic reduction was achieved by a restrictive control policy with minimal education or medical intervention. A social refusal of illicit recreational drug use prevailed in the country. A similar popular consensus supported the restrictive policies which rolled back cocaine epidemics in Germany, France and Switzerland after the First World War.[99]

I was one of the members of our Drug Commission to visit Spain in 1972. Francisco Franco some years before had established a policy

---

98 Gabriel Nahas, "Drugs, The Brain and the Law" a pamphlet published by the Notre Dame Journal of the Law, Vol. 5, Issue No. 3, Notre Dame, p. 740

99 Gabriel Nahas, op. cit. p. 73. All of the information so far in this No-Tolerance section is drawn from Dr. Nahas.

banning the recreational use of mind-altering drugs. The penalties were harsh. A person convicted of the possession of one marijuana cigarette, received a sentence of six years in jail. There were no shortened sentences for Spaniards or foreigners. The law was enforced. The people of Spain simply did not use the banned drugs. And the jails were not crowded.

We visited a young American who had served two of his six years in jail. He and a friend during their first three years as students in a renowned American university had come to believe that America was such a rotten place that they quit college to travel around the world to visit some of the "countries which were doing it right." Spain was their last stop. When he was asked which countries were the good ones, he said, "America is the best by far. Why don't you people in the colleges," he asked me, "tell the students the good things about our nation and help us appreciate them?"

In Spain, at that time, there was virtually no crime. Some women students from our college in Spain for their junior year, told us they could go anywhere in Madrid, day or night, without the slightest possibility of encountering a hostile act. Spain was virtually crime-free as well as drug-free. To be sure Spain's government was a dictatorship. Even so, one has to wonder if a nation without crime and without drugs might have some very valuable freedom that the free societies lack.

In 1982, after Franco died, the penalties for drug infractions were greatly reduced and possession for personal use was decriminalized. Four years later, The Chicago Tribune decided to learn the consequences of the liberalized laws. Madrid's Chief of Police told the reporters that there were 100,000 heroin addicts in Spain, 30,000 of them in Madrid, and crime in Spain had sky-rocketed, 75% of it drug-related. THE DRUG LEGALIZERS NEED TO STUDY THIS CASE HISTORY THOROUGHLY AND THOUGHTFULLY.

When our drug commission visited Greece in 1972, we learned, that apart from certain young people who had frequent contact with tourist youth, there wasn't much use of illegal recreational drugs in that country. In response to our questions about why the Greek people tended not to be drug-users, we received very much the same answers from clinicians, psychiatrists, doctors, law enforcement officials and government personnel. Most Greeks, they said, had strong family commitments, they respected the laws and they belonged to a church which insisted on standards of conduct.

The United States is Not Without its Own Success Stories

In 1981, a naval plane, heading back to its aircraft carrier, crashed on landing. There was no apparent reason for the accident. When the pilot's blood was tested, it turned out to contain a mind-altering drug. Shortly thereafter, a major survey across the Navy, conducted by one of the Big-Eight accounting firms, was ordered by the Chief of Naval Operations, Admiral Thomas Hayward, revealing upwards of 47% of naval personnel were using drugs both on duty and off. This led to the institution of a policy of zero-tolerance for illegal drugs by Admiral Hayward, to be applied to officers as well as enlisted personnel. The level of drug use in the U.S. Navy plummeted over the ensuing six months to under 7% and has been declining ever since. The no-tolerance policy remains in effect with commensurate results. There have been periodic, up-dated public reports of this accomplishment, but they received next to no coverage by the nation's news media.[100]

Another kind of remarkable success story in modern America took place in Missouri. "We are not a housing project! We are a neighborhood!" This was the declaration of Bertha Gilkey in an unforgettable television show in 1986. Bertha Gilkey is an African-American who led a successful battle against crime, drugs, vandalism, disrepair, filth, rats and vermin, transforming the Cochran housing development in St. Louis from a loathsome high-rise slum into a neatly-kept, safe, lawful and upbeat residential dwelling.

How did Bertha Gilkey and her associates accomplish this transformation? First, they obtained authorization from the Federal Government for the residents to manage the building. Then they applied their own common sense and enlisted the residents in drawing up rules to govern the behavior of the people living there. The new rules required the children to be properly supervised. Illegal drugs were forbidden. All apartments had to be kept in good repair, and all the tenants were required to take turns cleaning the public areas. Security guards were hired to police the premises.

The rules were enforced by elected officers who had the authority to evict a tenant who did not abide by the rules or whose children did

---

[100] Admiral Hayward verified this statement 2/2/05.

not. Applicants for an apartment were screened by a committee as to whether they measured up to the standards of upright and neighborly conduct. Before long there was an increasing waiting list of applicants for vacant apartments.

When Bertha Gilkey explained all this on television, the astonished host asked how they could possibly evict someone from public housing who used illegal drugs. She declared, "Public housing is not built for criminals and vandals and people who use illegal drugs!"

Our Drug Laws Haven't Failed!

The drug laws haven't failed. They have never been implemented. The leaders of the Cochran Housing Project adopted new policies and saw to it that they were carried out. And something close to a miracle occurred.

The United States Government, fulfilling its obligation under the United Nations Single Convention on Narcotic Drugs enacted laws prohibiting the use of marijuana, cocaine and opiates. But instead of arresting and punishing the users, the national government decided to concentrate on preventing the production of the drugs and intercepting and penalizing the traffickers. This endeavor has been an exercise in futility since the beginning, and one which has had tragic consequences for other nations as well as our own.

The problem is that the market works. As long as there are millions of Americans wanting, and many craving, the drugs, the huge sums of money to be made in providing the drugs will attract a limitless number of individuals willing to risk their freedom, and even their lives to deliver the goods. The government can go on forever increasing the number of coast guard boats, sniffing dogs, specially trained customs agents, reconnaissance planes and law enforcement teams, but the drug trade will continue to flourish.

In dealing with the issue of mind-altering drugs, as with family disintegration, the degradation of literature and entertainment, unwed motherhood and all the other social pathologies, the nation's leadership has been incapable of digging in its heels and saying "That's a bad thing and needs to be remedied." The dominance of the non-judgmental left in the entire range of opinion-making industries has stripped the gears of public moral judgment. Right and wrong have been driven from the marketplace of social discourse.

Consider, for example, the earnest effort of the National Council of Churches to address television's impact upon the viewers. In 1985, after two years of study, the conclusion was reached that "violence in the media does lead to aggressive behavior in children, teen-agers and adults who watch the programs." Strong measures were urged in the report. James Wall, the distinguished editor of the Christian Century, and Committee Chairman, warned that "the television industry must clean up its act to avoid censorship." Rev. Wall and his committee, hemmed in by the non-judgmental culture, made an end run around the problem it was supposed to address. Rather than chastising the television industry directly, they said if television didn't improve, the Federal Communications Commission would force it to do so.

So too, with the Federal Government's effort to enforce the drug laws. The policies avoided penalizing the drug users by going after the traffickers whom everyone knew were bad guys.

The standards of civil behavior which Bertha Gilkey resurrected and applied at the Cochran Housing Development had become casualties of a political illness which rages in most of the Western democracies. The essential and healthy tissues of civil rights metastasized into an unhealthy and uncontrollable growth that has displaced and overwhelmed the body politic, children's rights, students' rights, gay rights, criminals' rights, women's rights, pornographers' rights, animal rights, and numerous other formulations for protection and privilege have crowded out and atrophied the very notion of civic responsibility. Obligations to other people and to the common good are no longer of general concern. Indeed the triumph of the rights of people to do pretty much as they please has been so comprehensive that the nation has become virtually incapable of applying the principles freedom requires to defend itself against any of the social pathologies.

The effort to control drug use is undermined by the ideologically applied term "drug abuse." This implies some use is acceptable. The fact that marijuana use is illegal scarcely enters the thoughts or conversation about drug issues. Think how many rich and famous people openly use and admit to using various prohibited drugs. And use by the obscure as well as the famous is forcefully protected by an army of rights advocates. If someone makes a sensible suggestion that the students in a public school or the employees of a defense contractor be tested for drug use, the vigilant champions of rights-above-everything-else raise such a storm of public protest about the invasion of privacy and the police-state mentality that all but the most intrepid anti-drug workers will back off apologetically. The public's toleration of this single-minded assertion of rights is ravaging the nation's defenses against the meltdown of the social order.

The Woeful Impact of America's Drug Problem on Other Nations

When I served on the National Commission on Marijuana and Drug Abuse, commission members were twice scheduled to visit Turkey to try to persuade the government to develop a more effective plan for restricting the growth of opium poppies in that land. The poppies were a primary source of income for Turkish farmers. Both meetings were cancelled by the U.S. State Department for fear that sensitive U.S.—Turkish negotiations on another matter might be compromised by opening up the unwelcome issue of crop reduction. How, I wondered, could our government with a straight face put pressure on Turkey, or any other country, to force its people to stop earning a profit on drug crops, when it is incapable of, or unwilling to, compel American citizens to stop using the drugs? Such a request from the U.S. government reflects an astounding arrogance. The Turks were supposed to make sacrifices to solve U.S. problems? And yet we have been engaged in such negotiations with Mexico, Afghanistan, Turkey, Colombia and many other nations.

There is another dimension of our relationships with drug-producing countries which deserves the thoughtful consideration of conscientious Americans. In November of 1984, Jacques Cousteau and his son provided a heart-breaking report of how the demand for cocaine, largely from the United States, has caused very high rates of crime and corruption in the countries that grow the coca plant and has led to increasing cocaine addiction among the natives who for centuries had been using the drug in a mild and relatively harmless form. And cocaine isn't the only trouble. A March, 1980 article in Playboy cited a DEA estimate that Colombia's marijuana exports total 7 billion dollars.

The destabilization of their nations by the drug traffic had become so grievous that in August of 1984, the governments of Bolivia,

Colombia, Ecuador, Venezuela, Peru, Panama and Nicaragua issued a joint declaration condemning drug-trafficking as a crime against humanity. A follow-up article in the Knight-Ridder newspapers stated, "The drug problem has reached such proportions in Latin America, officials say, that it is threatening not only the economies, the social well-being and national health, but national stability as well."

A recent report presents a tragic and frightening tale of how extreme and virtually uncontrollable the drug scourge has become.

The August 8/27-28/11 issue of the Wall Street Journal, carried a front page feature article entitled, "Just An Ordinary Day of Death in Mexico's War on Drug Traffickers." This is the beginning of that article.

> A little past midnight on a recent Friday, Manuel Lopez, a twenty-six year-old lawyer, accidentally drives his Volkswagen into a gun battle between rival drug gangs in the tourist resort of Acapulco. As bullets tear into his car, he hits the brakes and tries to run. He makes it less than a yard before falling dead . . .
>
> Since President Felipe Calderón took office in December 2006, declaring war on traffickers, roughly 43,000 people have been killed in drug-related homicides.

America's national conscience has been virtually destroyed by the out-of-control drug scourge, thanks to higher education's rejection of its obligation to uphold public law, and to the enormous amount of money and influence invested by heartless billionaires like Soros, determined to eliminate anti-drug laws in the states so that all marijuana users may indulge their enjoyment of mind-altering drugs. The tragedy of Mexico's losing battle with murderous crime is primarily the direct result of America's insatiable demand for drugs and its failure to enforce anti-drug laws.

Conclusion

On June 8, 1998, a full-page letter to U.N. Secretary General Kofi Annan was published as an ad in the New York Times in advance of the U.N.'s special session on Drugs later in the week. The letter stated

"We believe that the global war on drugs is now causing more harm than the drug itself." A second, adjacent full-page ad listed the names and affiliations of some of the 500 signatures on the actual communiqué to Mr. Annan. The signatures appear to be drawn from a Who's Who of the rich and famous and influential from universities, corporations, clergy, state and national government, etc. It is difficult to identify any of them who have any particular knowledge of the matter they are endorsing. George Soros and his Lindesmith Center coordinated the undertaking. Mr. Soros is not only spending enormous sums of money in his attack on drug laws, he is using his larger-than-life stature and his extensive contacts to mobilize others for the cause.

The casual acceptance by the American society of the pervasive use of illegal, mind-altering drugs provides a red-alert echo of Meg Greenfield's deep concern about the collapse of moral authority in our nation. That the colleges and universities were the primary agencies for the national diffusion of the drug pestilence is appalling; and given the fact that mind-altering drugs impair intellectual activity, which one has to suppose is what colleges and universities engage in; the callous campus indifference to the social havoc America's widespread drug use causes in our own nation and many others, the academic community seems to be devoid of civic conscience. An additional testimony to that dismal condition occurred in April of 1999 when the National Association of Scholars conducted a symposium entitled "What is Higher Education's Responsibility to Society?" The Association's Chairman, Stanley Rothman, a Professor of History Emeritus of Smith College, introduced the program, noting that the symposium theme would not have commanded much attention among his generation of teacher scholars. For them the answer to the question was simple. "The university did not have any obligations to the larger society. It was an entity to itself."

The next speaker, Allen Kors, Chairman of the Department of History at the University of Pennsylvania, said that apart from obeying the laws, universities have no responsibilities whatever. Later, he stated "I joined the academic world not to meet any responsibilities to society, but to meet my responsibilities to myself."

The third speaker, Dennis O'Brien, who had served as President of the University of Rochester and also as president of Bucknell, said, "The medieval pattern of study and its latter-day successor, the classical curriculum of our nineteenth-century colleges are regarded as narrow, parochial and constrictive of academic freedom in the name of religious dogma . . . Rather than the medieval defense of dogma, modern higher education aims at dedogmatizing the student body."

This symposium and the rejection of all value judgments by the White House Task Force and the protection of the faculty's academic freedom as the top university purpose, all deliver the same message— American higher education no longer appears to be one of the basic institutions of the nation.

In April of 1999, Eric Harris and Dylan Kliebold, two well-to-do and apparently sane young men, planned and carried out the slaughter of fellow students at Columbine High School. A number of actions have been taken to try to protect students—adding security, officers, mobilizing national campaigns to tighten gun restriction and so on. They have been of no use because the problem was that the teen-age gunmen, to put it bluntly, were moral savages, incapable of recognizing and refraining from acts of absolute evil. They were also the hapless victims of a society that failed in its fundamental obligation to its children. Each society must train its youth to live responsibility in its own society.

It is now clear that much of higher education has seceded from the union. In 1976, Robert M. Hutchins, the former President of the University of Chicago and founder of the Center for the Study of Democratic Institutions, wrote an essay entitled, "Is Democracy Possible?" The following are excerpts from that commentary.

> *The aim of any democracy must be the common good . . . The exact opposite of democracy is government by pressure groups. This is a government under which special interests, by deals and propaganda, endeavor to exploit the community for their own benefit . . . A community is composed of diverse people with diverse interests. These people become a community through their dedication to the common good, or there will be no community . . .* [101] In view of the condition of our education, our mass media, and our political parties, the outlook for democracy, the free society, and the political community is not good.[102]

---

101 [Italics added]

102 Robert M. Hutchins, The Center Magazine, The Center for the Study for Democratic Institutions, Santa Barbara, Spring, 1976.

Alexander Solzhenitsyn also had misgivings about the future of America's free society. He gave the 1979 Commencement Address at Harvard University. "There are," he said, "telltale symptoms by which history gives warning to a threatened or perishing society. Such are, for instance, a decline of the arts, or a lack of great statesmen . . . The West has finally achieved the rights of man, but man's responsibility to God and to society has grown dimmer and dimmer . . . All the celebrated technological achievements of progress, including the conquest of outer space, do not redeem the twentieth century's moral poverty."

Both of those symptoms of a perishing society characterize America today. It is a nation split apart, separated by irreconcilable views of matters judged by both sides to be of utmost importance. The intensity of disagreement is so great that the national unity that surfaced briefly after 9/11 seems irretrievable. It is tragic and a matter for thoughtful people to ponder, that no great statesman has arisen to present a plan for reducing the contention and restoring the good will that for so many years delivered America's unmatched well-being and success.

Much of higher education has now become what Robert Hutchins described as "a pressure group struggling against all other pressure groups through deals and propaganda, to exploit the community for its own benefit" and sustaining that status surrounded by an impenetrable wall of academic freedom.

Like the student assassins at Columbine High School, several generations of professors and academic administrators, were never educated about their responsibilities in America's free society. They are unaware of its total dependence upon a virtuous populace, and the educational philosophy which addressed Aristotle's dictum that the educational system must reenforce the government. They have been heedlessly undermining and dismantling the uniquely successful program of education which had served America exceedingly well. Like the assassins at Columbine High School, the value-neutral educators haven't a clue about the devastation they are wreaking on their own society, nor, apparently, even a fragment of conscience about that devastation.

PART II

Thus far, this book has focused on the concepts and movements and individuals that contributed to the repudiation of the educational philosophy underlying the system of education that served America very well during the four centuries starting with the Plymouth Colony. Its foundational purpose was to shape the character of the students and fit them to live piously, honestly, patriotically, responsibly and cooperatively, as George Washington repeatedly urged them to do, in order to sustain their self-governing free society.

This part of the book presents my training, career, and experiences during the two decades from World War II until I reported for duty as President of Rockford College on February 1, 1960.

I was in my junior year at Princeton University when the Japanese bombed Pearl Harbor. My military service began in a camp in Texas that trained troops for duty in a tank battalion. Eventually, we were sent to England and groomed there for landing in France. From D-Day until the European war ended, we were under enemy fire a good part of the time. I doubt if any other mode of life can provide such a thorough understanding of human nature as enduring months and months of combat duty during which you live and work with the same people twenty-four hours a day. You come to know them better than you do the members of your own family.

Back in the United States, I enrolled at Northwestern University and earned a Bachelor of Science in Teaching and a Master of Arts in Counseling and Guidance. In 1947, I was hired as Dean of Students at a small private junior college that was being established in California. Later, I was appointed Vice President of the College. I became a good friend of Dr. Saunders, the president of the college, who had earlier presided over another college. I learned much from him about college administration. In those days, Americans were still family-oriented, religiously-rooted, patriotic, lawful and friendly. Serving a college at that time was a congenial vocation. We added the junior and senior years and achieved accreditation as a liberal arts college.

In 1955, I was appointed Executive Vice Chairman of President Eisenhower's Committee on Government Contracts, the ranking member of the staff. In those days racial discrimination persisted in much of America. President Eisenhower had issued an Executive Order, fulfilling an effort begun by President Truman, requiring companies that obtained government contracts to open jobs to qualified members of minority groups. One of my responsibilities was to find ways in which the Equal Job Opportunities Program could become better known.

We asked the Chicago Association of Commerce and Industry to poll their members and make a list of companies that already welcomed applicants from minority groups. We then held a conference for the high school guidance counselors of the Chicago area, and provided each guidance counselor with a copy of the list. They were amazed at how many companies were already open to minority applicants and regretted this information hadn't been made known much earlier.

In Detroit, our effort was to persuade a large union to open its membership to minority workers. That negotiation required some nudging from Washington, but the undertaking was successful. Both of these initiatives provided paradigms for other cities to follow.

The time with the committee provided an opportunity to become well-acquainted with various national leaders. I met periodically with Max Raab, the Secretary of the Cabinet, so that he could keep the President informed of our progress. Committee members with whom I conferred fairly frequently were William Rogers, the Attorney General [and later the Secretary of State]; Secretary of Labor James Mitchell; Mrs. Ogden Reid, publisher of the New York Herald Tribune, and Ivan Willis, Vice President of International Harvester. In the course of my work I had meetings with top corporate executives, labor leaders, and various national civil rights organizations.

During my time in Washington, I came to realize that the period after World War II was one of substantial cultural changes in America that were not widely understood. It was clear that a leader of any college determined to provide an education adapted to the free society, would need to have pondered major cultural changes in America, and I began to study them. The family-centered and religiously-rooted life which had characterized America was yielding to pressures that created a generation gap not only within the family, but in the whole society. During the war, many wives obtained jobs in defense industries, leaving children without parental love and guidance during the day. Often the children were of an age when parental involvement was needed for the development of social and emotional maturity. It was in this period that it became common for women to have jobs.

That transition combined with the far-reaching impact of the naïve and irrational 1947 Supreme Court Decision to remove God from education and, to a great extent, from the marketplace of ideas, resulted, as already noted, in a decisive decline in the percentage of American youth for whom religion was important in their lives and who attended church regularly.

In that era of fracturing families and diminishing religious impact, a youth culture emerged, shaking off and becoming hostile to the traditional standards of civilized behavior. In 1954, Elvis Presley surfaced and "by 1956, he was an international sensation. With a sound and style that uniquely combined his diverse musical influences, and blurred and challenged the social and racial barriers of the time. He ushered in a whole new era of American Music and pop culture."[103] Wikipedia, noted that "He became the leading figure in rock and roll . . . His uninhibited performance style made him enormously popular and controversial."[104]

The Beatles formed a rock group in 1960. "They are one of the most commercially successful and critically acclaimed acts in the history of popular music . . . The nature of their enormous popularity, which first appeared as "Beatlemania," transformed as their song-writing grew in sophistication. They came to be perceived as the embodiment of the ideals of the social and cultural revolutions of the 1960s."[105]

Before long rock music, and music far more crude and hostile to all of Christendom's behavioral standards, became an obsession, for

---

103 www.elvis.com/abouttheking/biography-.aspx

104 Wikipedia. 8/16/11

105 Wikipedia 8/11/11

America's youth. In many families, the dominance of rock music in the lives of the youth further damaged the already strained intergenerational communications and cordiality.

My first direct encounter with the radical and destructive phenomenon of rock music was in 1968 when I served as co-chairman of the Awards Program of The Freedoms Foundation at Valley Forge. After days of poring through the Awards entries, The Foundation provided us with an elegant dinner of appreciation. The after-dinner program was provided by a Colonel from the Pentagon. He apologized for the slide program he was going to show. It was the lyrics of the top ten rock music songs. In the aggregate, they delivered a shocking hostile attack on God, morality, the family, the government and the laws. The Colonel expressed deep concern at the Pentagon about whether troops immersed in the rock music culture could perform responsibly and intelligently as military personnel, and whether their emotional stability could sustain them in combat.

The young people growing up in the 1950's and 1960's became increasingly uneasy about the threat of atomic warfare. Bomb shelters were built and schools had occasional evacuation drills. There was much public distress about the rapid spread of Soviet Communism across the world. The East/West tensions took on the ominous title of "Cold War." As time went on the baby boom generation worried about the expansion of the Vietnam war, and the ever-growing number of draftees. Draft resistance urged on by radical professors became a badge of honor.

The increasing hostility of young people toward the free society's standards of conduct was dramatically brought into focus by a New York University Professor, Michael Blonsky, in a Chicago Tribune interview. His field of work was cultural trends. The interview took place in Nike Town, a glittering new store on Chicago's Michigan Avenue that sold wildly expensive sneakers. "This" said Blonsky on entering the store, "is a church! A post-modern church!" Then pointing to a life-size figure of Michael Jordan, the basketball star, he declared, "Look! There's God!" This was not just crude and blasphemous flippancy. He went on to explain that many people today are totally unpersuaded by any system of beliefs. For them, flashy shoes are as important as anything gets. Beyond a fascination with the ownership of impressive things, Blonsky cited as other key values of the New Culture: glamour, fitness, youth, power, freedom, eroticism, and violence. "In the 1960's and 1970's,"

Blonsky noted, "the human psyche began to be reordered, it got altered. The feeling is, people are being produced that are different from before World War II.

I realized it was time for me to return to my graduate studies. Since I had not sought the Washington appointment, and had completed the two years to which I was committed, I resigned from the Government Contract Committee to reenroll at Northwestern. There I was most fortunate to become acquainted with Dr. Thomas Palfrey, a professor of French Literature. One day he asked me about my plans for a career. I told him I hoped to become a college president. "You are talking to the right fellow," he said. "You should do your doctoral degree in French Literature and your dissertation on François Guizot. He is the ideal tutor for you." Guizot was a professor of history at the Sorbonne and founded the first journal devoted to educational matters. He wrote the lead editorial in each issue, drawing on the wisdom of educational analysts all the way back to classical Greece and Rome.

Guizot was elected to the French Parliament and drafted legislation to provide a system of national schools. When that bill was enacted, he was chosen to be Minister of Education to implement the program. Many years later, the British Government sent a delegation led by poet and scholar Matthew Arnold to try to learn why the French schools were so much more effective than the British ones. Virtually all of the school and government and church officials visited by the delegation gave the same answer. It was Guizot's influence that made the difference. In his educational journal and on through five decades of public service, Guizot insisted that the fundamental purpose of education is the moral and ethical development of the students. "A sound body, a righteous mind, and a virtuous character—these are what a good education must produce. This goal is invariable and universal." Thus began one of the first editorials in his educational journal.

For anyone who was an adult before World War II, it is hard to believe the people described by Professor Blonsky are from the same country as pre-war Americans, or even the same planet.

Fulfilling Aristotle's Requirement

The following commentaries illustrate the three essential elements of a college program needed to fill Aristotle's insistence that education be designed to support the nature of the society. In our self-governing free society those elements are: Christianity, the family and patriotism. Those three also address Montesquieu's declaration that the people of a free society must be virtuous.

The Christianity segment is the first chapter from my new book Christianity: Lifeblood of America's Free Society (1620-1945). The segment on family presents articles, speeches and quotations that bear on family life. The Patriotism section is a blend of articles, speeches and quotations. They are followed by a selection of speeches to help students and other audiences to think about important topics that usually receive only superficial analyses in opinion-forming presentations and are scarcely noticed by young people in this era of the generation gap. The final section of the book presents highlights from the seventeen years of my tenure at Rockford College.

CHRISTIANITY
A Glimpse of Christianity

First Chapter of Christianity: Lifeblood of America's Free Society (1620-1945) by John Howard

With the truly great people of the world, the greatness does not seem to be in them, but through them. What sets them apart are the noble ideals that shape their lives. Think of Mother Teresa in her unflagging ministry to the desperately poor in India. Malcolm Muggeridge tells of her response when she was asked how she hoped to succeed in such daunting circumstances. She replied that her effort was not to succeed, but to serve.

Think of the four chaplains on a torpedoed navy vessel on which there were not enough life-preservers who gave theirs to crew members, praying together as they went down with the ship.

Robert Coles, the Harvard psychiatrist, writes of his encounter with Ruby Bridges, a black first-grader who started attending a New Orleans school in 1960 after a Federal judge ordered the schools to integrate. Ruby, the only black child to enroll, was daily escorted by Federal marshalls into the school, and later out of the school, always through an angry, hostile crowd.

> She came out and the people started . . . They called her this and they called her that. They brandished their fists. They told her she was going to die and they were going to kill her . . . I wondered who was going to come out

> of the school next. But then I found out no one else was in the school. The school had been totally boycotted by the white population.[106]

In time, Dr. Coles became acquainted with Ruby and her family, and learned that although there were furious hecklers waiting for her morning and afternoon, the child seemed happy and well-adjusted. One evening, at the Bridges' home, Dr. Coles said the teacher had told him Ruby had talked to the street people that morning. Ruby replied she wasn't talking to them, but just saying a prayer for them.

> "Ruby, you pray for the people there?"
> "Oh, yes."
> "Why do you do that?"
> "Because they need praying for."
> "Ruby, why do you think they need you to pray for them?"
> "Because I should."[107]

With Mother Teresa, the chaplains and Ruby, it is the selflessness shining through their lives that is fixed in our memory.

Through many experiences during ninety years, I have come to believe that God has given every human being the potential to derive deep satisfaction from helping someone else. For many, that gift lies dormant, never put to use because of an environment poisoned by "me generation" suppositions. Even so, it can be activated by the right stimulus.

An example of this inborn kindness occurred in Belgium on Christmas Day, 1944. I was in a tank battalion, part of the First Infantry Division, on the north flank of the Battle of the Bulge. We were deployed in an east-west line to try to prevent the Nazis from driving north to the huge supply depots in the port cities. A persistent fog dimmed our view of retreating American troops on the road in front of us. Bursts of machine gun and artillery fire heightened the tension. I was standing in the turret beside our gunner. Suddenly, he poked me in the ribs and gasped, "Look at that!"

I whirled around. A girl, perhaps nine years old, was approaching our tank. She told us that the people of the village had fled their homes

---

106 Robert Coles, Finding God at Harvard, Kelly Monroe, ed., p. 35, Zondervan, Grand Rapids, 1996.

107 Coles, Ibid., p. 37.

as the shooting war returned to the area. She had stayed behind to try to care for her invalid grandfather. She said they had run out of food and wondered if we had any to spare. Our crew immediately gave her the rations we had in the tank. She put them in the make-shift basket of her apron. Then she looked up and said, "Oh! Thank you! Thank you! It is a wonderful Christmas after all!" The surprising thing is that the five of us in the tank also felt it was a wonderful Christmas. That spontaneous act of helpfulness opened a window of warm cheer in that bleak morning of battlefield tensions.

Working against that generous impulse is the whole range of natural instincts that are fired up by any threat to our health or safety, our possessions, our satisfactions and pleasures, our self-image, our beliefs and prejudices, our family and friends, our livelihood, and our routines or whatever we are inclined to do. Human beings are touchy and sensitive and selfish. In the natural state, untamed and untrained, they tend to engage in an every man for himself struggle, the condition Thomas Hobbes described as the war of all against all.

All those self-serving emotions make it difficult for people to live and work together unless they are restrained by laws and rules, or by tradition, or by religious teachings. At the time Jesus lived, brutality and authorized killing were a part of daily living, a not surprising circumstance since Rome had conquered the known world and its troops were stationed in the cities of the lands bordering the Mediterranean Sea. Julius Caesar's nephew, Augustus, was the Emperor. The entertainment drawing the largest audiences occurred in the amphitheaters where gladiators fought. When one got the upper hand, the emperor, or whoever was the ranking official, would decide whether the dominant warrior should kill his opponent. Sometimes, for the enjoyment of the audience, criminals were put into the arena to be killed by wild beasts.

In the Roman religion, the temple of Vesta, one of the goddesses, was kept by six virgins. If any of them broke her vows of chastity and service to the temple, she was buried alive in a public ceremony. In the Jewish religion women found guilty of adultery were stoned to death by the people. Individuals guilty of certain crimes were nailed to a cross, ultimately dying after a long period of agony. These crucifixions drew large audiences. When Herod ordered all the male children under the age of three to be put to death, it was a tragic slaughter, but the Bible does not report any public revolts.

The Roman calendar had almost a hundred holidays. They had multiplied as the cosmopolitan Romans came to know about, and became followers of gods worshipped in places they had conquered. Among them were the Egyptian goddess, Isis, and Mithras, the Persian god of life and truth, and Cybele the Phrygians' mother goddess. Her celebrations involved frenzied dancing. A number of the holidays were occasions for drunken sexual orgies. The Saturnalia, a word still used to identify such a festivity, lasted several days during which nobody worked. Emperor Augustus became so concerned about the wild behavior of the people that he urged them to return to the worship of traditional Roman gods, but that did not happen.

Among the Jews, their religious faith was beset by a number of rival sects, each claiming to be the protectors and spokesmen for the only right interpretation of what Jehovah required of His people. Returning after seventy years of exile in Babylon, the Jews found that the Temple in Jerusalem had been destroyed. Public worship had been discontinued. A revival of their religious services required the guidance of scholars steeped in the ancient laws of their faith. The Scribes were the leaders of this effort. Houses of Assembly were established where the Scribes officiated at worship and instruction. Different groups of Scribes reached different conclusions about the laws with the result that other religious sects emerged urging the people to accept their views. These sects included the Pharisees, the Sadducees, the Essenes, the Zealots and the Nazarites, all with their own interpretations and priorities. Some of the sects were openly and aggressively hostile to others.

Into that age of barbaric cruelty and heated religious antagonism, came a young, unknown carpenter from an obscure village preaching humility and brotherly love. PREACHING WHAT?? A life governed by such motives was at that time simply unimaginable to the people of Palestine, regardless of their religious faith, their nationality, or their station in life. Such ideas didn't even exist. For Jesus to have succeeded at all in his mission is, itself, proof of his divinity.

His preparation for his ministry was unique. Until he was thirty, he lived an ordinary life among ordinary people. After this prolonged opportunity to experience what it was to be a human being, he reported for duty, presenting himself to John The Baptist for the ceremony in which he dedicated himself to God. As the first step in that commitment, he went into the wilderness for forty days of fasting and prayer. At the end of that meditation when his body was weakened by the lack of nourishment, Satan appeared and urged him to satisfy his hunger by turning stones into bread. When Jesus refused, Satan took him to the top of the Temple and said, "Jump off, and prove you are divine as you are rescued by an angel." Again, the answer was "No." So Satan, knowing the human lust for power, took him to a mountain top looking out over the earth and said, "If you will worship me, I will give you control of all the kingdoms of the world." For the third time, Jesus refused.

After the long period of observing human life, and after withstanding Satan's best efforts to tempt him physically, mentally and spiritually, Jesus began his preaching as God's son. He was quickly perceived as a voice of authority, speaking with words and illustrations that engaged the interest of an audience. That interest was keenly intensified as he promised eternal life to all who would live according to his teachings. The possible truth of that astonishing promise was greatly reinforced by Jesus' miraculous cures for the diseased and the physically disabled. As word spread about this powerful new evangelist, many would gather to hear him wherever he went.

When a particularly large crowd assembled, Jesus climbed a hill to give what became known as The Sermon on the Mount, in which he touched on many of the subjects later addressed throughout his ministry. It is significant that he began with an assurance that what he had to say was for everybody. He wanted the meek and the persecuted to know that they were as important to God as anyone else, indeed, that because their humble lives seemed to be insignificant, they would receive special rewards in Heaven. What a shocker that was! These Beatitudes very appropriately are the lead-in to Jesus first recorded homily.

After touching on several topics, Jesus offers instruction on how to pray, beginning "Our Father . . ." That "our" spreads open arms to everyone. All human beings are God's beloved children. "Give us this day our daily bread." This is not a remote and superior God, concerned only with matters of supreme importance. He is a God who cares about the everyday needs of each human being. Wealthy people would never give a thought to finding the next meal, but many people must, and Jesus makes it plain that God knows and cares about such matters.

Early in The Sermon, Jesus said, "Think not that I am come to destroy the law, or the prophets: I am come not to destroy, but to fulfill." Quickly, however, he makes it clear that his concept of how best to fulfill the Judaic Laws is completely different from what had always been assumed. "Ye have heard that it was said by them of old time, thou shalt not commit adultery: But I say unto you, that whosoever looketh on a woman to lust after her hath committed adultery with her already in his heart." What has happened here? In The Ten Commandments the person is told to do certain things and not to do certain other things. Behavior was controlled by an outside authority. Abiding by God's instructions was righteous. Defying these instructions was sinful. One's behavior was to be governed by an external force.

Jesus, here in his first recorded teaching, is telling people that what they think and say and do is not to be determined by a code of religious instructions. His message is, "God, through me, is announcing a far better system for governing your lives." Actually, it is a very simple and very powerful system. It is one which, when learned and completely put into practice, will provide unfailing guidance for every circumstance. Instead of trying to get this message across all at once, Jesus just offers several illustrations of the system. A married person should avoid sexual activity with anyone other than the married partner, but that faithfulness should occur because the person's whole life has been transformed by loving-kindness. Love for a husband or wife would rule out any thought of taking up with someone else. Here, the motive for not lusting after another, comes from within and it is the positive and loving protection of one's marriage, not the stern duty to avoid adultery, that determines the matter.

Another illustration Jesus offers, one even more surprising than the motive for avoiding adultery is, "Ye have heard that it hath been said that Thou shalt love thy neighbor, and hate thine enemy. But I say unto you, Love your enemies, bless them that curse you, do good to them that hate you, and pray for them that despitefully use you, and persecute you; that ye may be children of your Father which is in heaven, for he maketh the sun to rise on the evil and on the good, and sendeth rain on the just and on the unjust."[108]

---

108 The Holy Bible, King James Version, Matt. 5:43-45

In this instance, Jesus is once again emphasizing that all human beings, even the cruel ones, are God's children so that a person totally engaged in spreading loving-kindness will suppress whatever natural antagonisms arise and be helpful in any way he can to those by whom he has been wronged. Forgiveness is one of the recurring emphases of Jesus' ministry.

The instruction to forgive had registered with the Apostle Peter, but such an action was so completely contrary to human nature that he wanted a little wiggle room. He asked Jesus how long a person should continue to forgive someone who wronged him again and again. "As many as seven times?" he asked. Jesus must have been disappointed that Peter had thought this was just a partial obligation, for he replied rather abruptly that Peter should forgive a person for seventy times seven offenses.

The fundamental importance of this Christian duty was fixed for all time when Jesus on The Cross urged God, "Forgive them for they know not what they do." Later on, the first Christian martyr, Saint Stephen, echoed Jesus' appeal to God. When he was being stoned to death, "he kneeled down, and cried with a loud voice, 'Lord, lay not this sin to their charge.'"[109]

Another matter of primary concern to Jesus was humility. It is essential to the Christian way of life. It will be recognized that any sense of self-importance gives rise to expectations that other people must acknowledge your status and behave accordingly. Self-importance, or egotism, is a breeding ground for hurt feelings, and thus a barrier to genuine and complete forgiveness. It also inclines the person to feel superior to some other people. In Christianity, there is no place for snobbery, no place for actions taken to impress people. In the Sermon on the Mount, Jesus tells his hearers that they should not pray or give gifts or engage in fasting in a manner that would call attention to their personal acts of devotion.

True humility and loving kindness combine in a life of service to other people. At The Last Supper, when the meal was concluded, Jesus poured water into a basin, and washed the feet of all the disciples. When he had finished, he said to them, "Know ye what I have done to you? Ye call me Master and Lord; and ye say well; for so I am. If I then, your

---

[109] The Holy Bible, op. cit., Acts 7:60

Lord and Master, have washed your feet; ye also ought to wash one another's feet. For I have given you an example, that ye should do as I have done to you."[110]

The person given over to helping others will naturally avoid another activity condemned by Jesus—passing judgment on other people. In the Sermon on the Mount, he uses the illustration of criticizing someone for having a speck in his eye when the fault-finder has larger problems of his own. Any fool can think up things that are wrong and make a big fuss about it. Some people make a whole career out of complaints. It takes intelligence and a kind heart to create a friendly and peaceable society, by discovering ways to cooperate with other people, whatever their short-comings.

Actually, Jesus was wholly realistic about the great range of natural impulses that incline a person toward actions contrary to his teachings. He knew from the beginning that all twelve disciples had their failings, but he patiently guided their apprenticeship. Just as he had spent thirty years learning about human life and human behavior, the disciples, in their sometimes fumbling ways, had spent three years learning about Jesus' concept of serving God. Then, after Jesus had risen, and after the disciples had been empowered by the Holy Spirit to work miracles and preach with authority, they had a direct knowledge of Jesus ministry to draw upon.

Many of the people whom Jesus healed had been leading lives far short of admirable—beggars, greedy tax-collectors, prostitutes, thieves—but when he realized they had faith in him, he forgave them and then healed them. The Christian promise of redemption and life eternal is open to everyone who seeks forgiveness and embraces Jesus as Lord and Savior, no matter what troubles or unchristian attitudes had previously marked his life.

In the Sermon on the Mount, the subject to which Jesus gives the most extensive treatment is directing the individual's primary attention to leading a godly life. "Lay not up for yourselves treasures upon earth where moth and rust doth corrupt and where thieves break through and steal: but lay up for yourselves treasures in heaven; where neither moth nor rust doth corrupt; and where thieves do not break through and steal: For where your treasure is, there will your heart be also . . . No man can

---

110 The Holy Bible, op. cit., John 13:12-15

serve two masters: for either he will hate the one, and love the other; else he will hold to the one, and despise the other. Ye cannot serve God and mammon." Mammon is the personification of riches, wealth, greed and a fixation on possessions. Jesus goes on to warn against an excessive concern for food and clothing as additional obstacles to serving God.

The all-inclusive definition of leading a godly life was set forth in Mark 12 when a scribe asked Jesus "which is the first commandment of all?" Jesus replied, "The first of all commandments is, Hear, O Israel: The Lord our God is one Lord: And thou shalt love the Lord thy God with all thy heart and with all thy soul, and with all thy mind, and with all thy strength: this is the first commandment. And the second is like, namely this, thou shalt love thy neighbor as thyself. There is none other commandment greater than these."

Here Jesus provides conclusive proof that his ministry is not a denial of the ancient Jewish law, for the first commandment Jesus enunciated is a word for word quotation from Deuteronomy 6:4, 5, and the second commandment, from Leviticus 19:18. As Paul states in Romans 13:10, "Love is the fulfilling of the law."

In 1890, a small book was published entitled *The Greatest Thing in the World.* It remained a best-seller for a long time. The author was Henry Drummond, a Scottish author and theologian. He lectured at colleges throughout Australia and America and became a colleague of Dwight Moody in his evangelical missionary tours. His book, actually one of his lectures, is an analysis of the thirteenth chapter of I Corinthians which begins, "Though I speak with the tongues of men and of angels and have not charity, I am become as sounding brass, or a tinkling cymbal." Drummond has judged that the proper translation throughout the passage should be "love" instead of "charity." He then considers each aspect of love cited by Paul. The person wholly committed to Christian love is long-suffering, kind, not envious nor greedy, not self-important nor obnoxious, is even-tempered and avoids evil and sin. After considering various aspects of love, Paul concludes his statement, "Now abideth faith, hope and love: these three; but the greatest of these is love.

Christian loving-kindness has a unique power to sustain people through the most tragic and devastating circumstances which natural disasters or human cruelty can deliver. Ernest Gordon, in his book Through the Valley of the Kwai, illustrates that amazing human capacity in his report about Japanese prison camps in World War II. The Japanese forced their underfed, ill clothed, diseased prisoners to build a railroad in extreme heat. The guards taunted and tortured and killed the prisoners for entertainment, as the Romans once did.

> When we did not move fast enough to suit them [the guards], which was most of the time, they beat us. Many no longer had the heart to endure such beatings. They slid to the ground and died . . . A guard enraged over some trifle, would shriek a curse, then hurl a hammer at the prisoner's head. A Japanese engineer carefully instructed two prisoners in making ready a dynamite charge. Then, while they were carrying out his instructions, he touched off the charge and blew them up . . . Everywhere men collapsed in their tracks, from thirst, exhaustion, disease and starvation . . . Existence had become so miserable . . . that nothing mattered except to survive . . . When a man lay dying, we had no word of mercy. When he cried out for help, we averted our heads . . . The atmosphere in which we lived was increasingly poisoned by selfishness, hatred and fear . . . Hate, for some was the only motive for living! We hated the Japanese.[111]

Ernest Gordon writes of a prisoner from his Scottish regiment who gave all his meals to his close friend to help him to get well. And then the generous helper died from starvation and exhaustion. In another instance, at the end of a day's cruel work on the railroad, the prisoners turned in their tools. The guard counted them and declared that a shovel was missing. The guard became uncontrollably angry and demanded that the guilty one step forward to be punished. When no one did, the

---

111 Ernest Gordon, Through the Valley of the Kwai, Bantam Books, Harper and Row, Publishers, New York, 1969, pp. 59, 64, 67. [This book has been republished by Zondervan Publishing House under the title, "To End All Wars."]

guard raised his rifle, aimed at the work detail and yelled, "All die! All die." A prisoner stepped forward and said, "I did it." The guard killed him brutally. When they returned to camp, the tools were counted again at the guard house and none was missing. As the stories of these two men circulated among the prison camps, other instances of sacrifice surfaced, and the hatred gave way to a growing pride in the heroic acts of self-sacrifice and a sense that life was worth living. Eventually Christian services were established. The prisoners went out of their way to help one another and the sense of hopelessness was replaced by an atmosphere of helpfulness.

Later in the book, Ernest Gordon reports on an incident in which the prisoners were being transported to another camp. Their train had been pulled off on a siding adjacent to carloads of very seriously wounded Japanese soldiers. They were filthy, covered with mud and blood, having received no medical treatment or care of any kind.

> They had been discarded as expendable, the refuse of war. They were more cowed and defeated than we had ever been.
>
> Without a word, most of the officers in my section unbuckled their packs, took out a part of their ration and a rag or two, and with water canteens in their hands, went over to the Japanese train . . . to give water and food and to clean and bind up the wounds.
>
> An allied officer from another section of the train said to me, "What fools you are!"
>
> Ernest Gordon said something about the good Samaritan.
>
> "But that's different . . . That's in the Bible. These are the swine who have starved and beaten us. These are our enemies." . . .
>
> I regarded my comrades with wonder. Eighteen months ago they would have joined readily in the destruction of our captors. Now these same officers were dressing the enemy's wounds. We had experienced

> a moment of grace there in those blood-stained railway cars.[112]

Forgiveness. Humility. Service to others. Love your enemies. Those who had created a church in the midst of extreme cruelty and despair had come to understand that God is love. For those war-torn prisoners, that inner spark of loving-kindness had become a light to guide their lives.

This transformation of the prisoners burning with hatred for the Japanese and resigned to a desperate existence of brutal maltreatment to confident men with a willingness to sacrifice their lives for other prisoners and to help their enemies was, I believe, the achievement of the Peace of Christ.

At the Last Supper, Jesus had said to the disciples, "Peace I leave with you. My peace I give to you." That is a startling promise. In the coming years of their ministry, the disciples would encounter hostility, threats, imprisonment, torture and even death. The history of their evangelism was anything but peaceful. However, just after bestowing peace upon them, Jesus said, "Not as the world giveth, give I unto you. Let not your heart be troubled, neither let it be afraid.[113] The peace of Jesus was not a harmony among individuals or groups. It was, instead, an armor of spiritual protection against whatever might trouble the heart or cause fear. It was a Peace of God which, as Paul stated, "is far more wonderful than the human mind can understand."[114] It was an inner serenity, a steady, tranquil peace of mind that would see them calmly through any torments or afflictions. Paul said, "I have learned in whatsoever state I am, therewith to be content."[115]

It is logical that Jesus should not have mentioned this peace until the Last Supper. It is a gift only available to those who have come to embrace the full reach of Christian loving-kindness, and the disciples were still learning about that until Jesus died. Moreover, after Jesus had risen and the disciples would be going out on their own to spread the Gospel, that is when they would have great need of Christ's peace.

---

112 Ernest Gordon, op.cit., pp. 178-9.

113 The Holy Bible, op. cit. John 14:27

114 The Living Bible, Tyndale House, Wheaton, Ill., 1982, Philippians 4:7

115 The Holy Bible, op. cip. Philippians 4:11

When Jesus appeared to the disciples for the last time, again he said, "Peace be with you."

FAMILY

A 1980 Gallup Poll showed that in America the family was the most important element in the lives of most Americans by a ratio of nine to one.

The Geneva Declaration issued by the World Congress of Families in 1999 states, "The natural family is the fundamental social unit, inscribed in human nature, and centered on the voluntary union of a man and a woman in the lifelong covenant of marriage." Further, at that Geneva Congress, Rabbi Jacob Neusner stated that the natural family—father, mother, children—is ordained by God and is so totally the centerpiece of human life that it is only by using the family as a metaphor that Jews and Christians even know how to talk about God, God as father and human beings as His children. "The family," he noted, "predates all other associations and institutions and is more important than all the others, including government, and must take precedence over all others."

> In recent years, nearly every line of social and psychological research points to the family as the foremost influence . . . in character formation, cultural education or upbringing . . . The family is the only social institution that is present in every single village, tribe, people or nation-state we know throughout history . . .
>
> There was a kind of family stability in the late 1940's and early 1950's . . . The divorce rate was quite low and fewer than 4% of all children born in America were illegitimate . . . Television, which became commercially available in 1948 was almost unknown. Popular magazines wrote of "togetherness," and radio soap operas featured families.[116]

[116] Cornell University Uri Branfenbrenner, "The Calamitous Decline of the American Family," The Washington Post, 2 January 1977.

> One of the most fascinating statistics in New York is the tiny number of intact families receiving welfare. As of July, 1981, 3700 intact families were receiving assistance from the HFDC program, and 4150 from general assistance, or less than 1% of all intact families of three or more persons in the city. [Emphasis added][117]

In the Christian faith, it is within the family that God made himself physically known to human beings in the earthly presence of His son, a revelation which dwarfs all other events of human history. As poet Mary Glew Penn wrote, "Time split in two that starry night and history fell apart." God made the family the core of human experience, and He made that primacy known beyond any doubt. In the instructions about how to live, which God gave Moses on Mount Sinai, the family was given the highest priority. Immediately following the listing of a person's obligations to God, came the Commandment to honor one's father and mother. That requirement was of even greater importance than "Thou shalt not kill."

The Christmas story, itself, reaffirms the priority of the family in human affairs. God could have presented His son as a full-grown teacher. God chose, instead, to give us the Divine Presence within a family.

In the Christendom brought by the Pilgrims to America, life revolved around the family as it continued to do, on through three centuries. It was largely through the experience of living within a family that children learned responsible and cooperative behavior.

"The kid who isn't loved knows it. There is no trauma so excruciating as parental rejection. No other form of human cussedness can more efficiently ruin a human life."

Jenkin Lloyd-Jones

The following is quoted from a feature editorial in the 1/8/93 issue of the Wall Street Journal.

---

117 Blanche Bernstein, The Politics of Welfare, p. 154, Abt Books, Cambridge, MA, 1982.

A trawl through the research data, compiled by scholars of left, right and center, yields horrifying findings. Young adults from disrupted families are more than twice as likely as adults from intact families to have sought psychiatric help; they are twice as likely to drop out of high school. Only one child in six of American children from divorced families sees his or her father as often as once a week; close to half had not seen their father within the past year.

On a material level, the income of mothers and children declines by an average of 30% following divorce, while the income of fathers rises by an average of 10% to 15%. Almost half of single mothers remain on the welfare rolls for over 10 years, and the children of those women are far more likely to remain on welfare for their adult lives.

Some 70% of juvenile criminals come from fatherless homes. The correlation between family makeup and poor discipline in school is so strong that it virtually erases any link to income, race or other factors.

. . . OUTRAGED BY SILENCE

Commencement Address
Brigham Young University
Provo, Utah
Aril 23, 1976
Dr. John A. Howard, President
Rockford College

Members of the class of 1976:

A chronological quirk has given to you and me some unusual opportunities. You are privileged to launch a second century for this sturdy university, and a third century for our cherished and somewhat confused nation. From today henceforth, by your works you can prove that the era now beginning can be one of hope and dignity. You can prove that courage and virtue are once again equal to the task of rigorous pioneering.

For my part, I have my own small anniversary to observe. Twenty-five years ago this month I was named president of a college. My opportunity is to distill from that quarter-century of experience a message sufficiently striking to penetrate the emotions of your graduation, and sufficiently wise and explicit to serve as a proper culmination for your studies and a remembered challenge in the years ahead. May we both measure up to these tasks.

The pioneers who came to Utah to bring a righteous civilization to a wilderness, and to convert barren deserts into fruitful farms and thrifty towns had no illusions about the work they set out to accomplish. They were fortified in their hearts for the hazards and the cruel frustrations they were to encounter. Their triumph stands as a glorious testimonial to a people powered by faith and guided by piety.

The work that faces your generation is no less arduous. The deserts you must bring to blossom are no less arid, but your mission may demand even more of you, for unlike the early pioneers of this state, you are confronted by a wilderness that is subtle and fluid and elusive. Indeed the wilderness you must conquer is disguised as a civilization so that there is the double necessity to unmask the deceit, to distinguish between what is authentic and what is counterfeit, so that you may labor to support the one and oppose the other.

I speak, of course, of the wilderness of unprincipled behavior into which our nation has wandered. The moral wasteland stretches from coast to coast, with only a few oases of righteousness here and there. The noble promise of America, the dream of a nation under God, which brought the Pilgrims to Massachusetts and which was confirmed in the Declaration of Independence, has been obscured and distorted and negated. That dream is today mocked and degraded by many of the most powerful forces in our society.

It is not a small challenge which I pose to you, but then you are not without special qualifications to meet it. When the invitation to speak at this ceremony was conveyed to me by President Oaks, I was greatly honored. I was also greatly pleased, for I recognized that for a person who earnestly cares about the future of this country—and I do—there are few audiences of such beneficent potential for our nation as a graduating class of Brigham Young University. I believe there is no single large group of your generation in the United States as consistently trained in its religious obligations, as ready to work long hours and make sacrifices for its principles, and as well versed in the dignity of self-reliance as you are. If that estimate is correct, you are greatly blessed and highly privileged.

I would not, however, want that flourish of admiration which is, I assure you, very genuine to go to your heads. It must be remembered that "unto whom much is given, of him much shall be required." The special assets of character which you possess seem to be so scarce in our land that if morality, integrity and piety are once again to become widely respected, the few people who do understand and cherish these fundamentals are going to have to work overtime, and with a rare degree of persistence, intelligence and humility.

Hercules, when first setting eyes on the Augean stables could not have been more appalled by the mess that confronted him than a conscientious American scrutinizing the contemporary scene. The moral depravity of what appears on television is rivaled by the moral tone of many campuses where cohabitation is a commonplace and where the use of illegal drugs does not even raise an eyebrow. The swelling tide of crime is matched by the deluge of dishonesty on the part of politicians who callously promise what they know they cannot deliver, and try to deceive the people into believing that projects can always be paid for out of someone else's pocket. Wherever one looks, a narrow concern for self-advantage seems to prevail over any thought of the well-being of the society, principles seem to be overwhelmed by expedience.

The person who may wish to involve himself in reestablishing principle as the guide for public and private conduct, may benefit from some perspective on the events of the last decade during which a slow-moving decline of character in our country has developed into an avalanche. It may be difficult for your generation to conceive what our society was like a scant ten years ago. Gutter language was rare on public platforms and in plays and movies. Coeducational dormitories were unthinkable. Most people had little worry about being out on the city streets late at night. Salacious literature was not publicly available on the news stands and in the bookstores, and marihuana was used by just a few people, mostly jazz musicians, migrant workers and a handful of silly socialites.

The revolutionaries who launched their Blitzkreig against our nation from the Berkeley campus may not have known how fragile our society was or how shallow were the moral commitments of America, but they seemed to understand with devastating precision how to cleave our people into hostile factions internally and how to paralyze our will to defend our principles abroad. By appealing to the passions and the fears of the young they were able to shred the fabric of self-restraint which alone binds a free civilization together. By glorifying the right to pleasure one's self, they swept away the respect for legitimate and responsible authority which is necessary for the cohesion and coordination of any group.

The radical quartet of filthy speech, marihuana, sexual liberation, and defiance of the military draft lured young people onto the shoals of personal and public anarchy where no rules or laws were acknowledged other than their own whims and passions. Although only a small percentage of the nation's youth completely accepted the call, few there were who were altogether immune to its invitation. The do-your-own-thing philosophy has spread throughout the country. It has toppled such venerable institutions as the campus honor system. This group technique for maintaining integrity, which had operated on many campuses, called upon every student to take some of the responsibility for making sure that no student cheated in his examinations. The priority now placed upon permitting each person to make his own judgments without regard to group norms has turned traditional values inside out, so that the act of "ratting" on another student is now regarded as more offensive than the act of cheating. In many places, the honor system which was once a manifestation of honorable people working together has been discarded. The old concept of honor based on integrity has yielded to a new code of honor based on dishonesty, also known as honor among thieves, which is, in fact, the source of the term "ratting."

The do-your-own-thing philosophy is, by definition, anti-social. Its partisans automatically disqualify themselves from effective membership in any formal group. If a person actually lives according to the belief that there are no restrictions upon his conduct other than what he chooses for himself, that person is in actuality a barbarian. The nightmare stories of the SLA and the Manson family make it clear that there are in America today genuine 24-karat barbarians, who have carried this depraved philosophy all the way to its ultimate degree of evil.

There is one particularly virulent aspect of this cancerous philosophy which needs to be recognized. The person who is only somewhat contaminated, who still has some moral sensitivities, is caught in a trap by his partial commitment. If he insists on the right to make his own decisions free of external authority, he is logically bound to champion the right of other people to do the same. Thus, he may find himself shielding and covering for other people in their commission of acts which he abhors. The phenomenon of multiplying vandalism clearly is dependent for some of its growth on the silence of many who know about the acts of destruction and deplore them, but say nothing. The malignancy feeds on itself. The deeds which are openly tolerated are becoming more and more bestial, and the limitations which once restrained barbarism are atrophying, while the so-called "liberation movements" are multiplying.

Well, what is to be done? Let us begin by reminding ourselves of a very simple moral fact. It was well phrased by the Swiss author, Henri

Frederic Amiel. "Truth," he said "is violated by falsehood, but it is outraged by silence." The abandonment of principle has of course been hurried along by false prophets preaching erroneous doctrine, but that fateful trend has been accelerated at least as much by worthy citizens who know better and sit quietly on the sidelines. Shakespeare observed in *King Henry VI*, "A little fire is quickly trodden out which, being suffered, rivers cannot quench."

Far too many religious people of our country, clergymen and laymen, mute and inactive, have suffered the arsonists of self-indulgence to put the torch to one sacred principle after another until we now face a general conflagration. As already noted, the task is a large one, but that is no cause for dismay: the works of lasting importance are never easy.

In calling upon you to rise to this circumstance and carry an oversize share of the responsibility, I have noted the particularly fortunate environment you have here at Brigham Young University. This campus is truly one of the few oases of righteousness. I recognize, however, that that blessing may also pose for you certain barriers that may not loom so prominent for the general citizenry. The devout person, knowing all too well his own shortcomings, is called upon not to pass judgment on others. This altogether commendable trait is to some extent reenforced by the First Amendment of our Constitution, which asserts the right of each citizen to proclaim his own views, whatever they are. It may then appear that the conscientious citizen is barred from speaking out against the doctrines that to him seem evil and against the advocates of those doctrines who are misleading the people.

We need to remember that although Jesus admonished the scribes and Pharisees not to stone the adulteress unless they, themselves, were without sin, still He commanded the woman to sin no more. To be charitable about the weaknesses of another person does not require silence about misdeeds. Furthermore, the First Amendment was never intended to prevent public discussion, nor to silence the virtuous citizens.

We seem, however, to be caught in a circumstance where the spokesmen who are opposed to our traditional religious and civic virtues are either greater in number than their opposites, or else are given more opportunities to be heard and read. That situation will persist until enough worthy and intelligent people decide they will no longer permit truth to be outraged by their silence. The citizen who is offended by the literature displayed in the grocery store where he does his shopping has only himself to blame if he fails to communicate his distress to the proprietor, and if he fails to encourage his friends to do the same. The viewer who considers certain television programs beyond the reasonable limits of public acceptability is abetting the problem if he does not write the sponsor, particularly now that one can obtain a complete list of the addresses of national television advertisers. The parent who finds wholly inappropriate certain subject matter in his children's classes has an obligation to make known his concern to the school authorities.

To a very great extent, the degeneration of public standards of conduct, and the increasingly corruptive character of literary, artistic and dramatic works are simply the result of what the citizens tolerate without voicing their strong objections. Like the small child who keeps going a little farther to see how much he can get away with, the pacesetters of the news and entertainment industries seem impelled to reach deeper and deeper into the cesspools of sensationalism, animalism and degradation. Their success is only possible because of the tolerance of those who know better. We must bear in mind that in public matters, there is no such thing as moral neutrality. Those who do not stand up forthrightly in behalf of their convictions, by their inaction are supporting the opposite view. On any scale wherever a person perceives right and wrong, silence turns out to be a vote for wrong.

Let us turn the coin over. The mission which lies before us is two-fold. The re-civilizing of America will not be accomplished merely by taking responsible action to discourage that which is vicious and decadent. We must proclaim the good news and make known to others that which is pure and worthy and wholesome and inspirational. Along with evangelism for one's religious beliefs, in which the Mormons need no advice and encouragement from outsiders, there must be a comparable evangelistic effort in secular matters. If a political officeholder takes a firm stand for some worthy cause in the face of contrary gusts of passion, write him and thank him and send a few copies of your letter off to other officeholders who need to recognize that courage and integrity are appreciated. If the publications you read are inclined to review only books of a sleazy and degrading character, write a letter to the editor with your own review of some book of hope and dignity, perhaps Corrie Ten Boom's *The Hiding Place*, or Ralph Moody's *Man of the Family*, or Russel Kirk's *The Roots of American Order*. If a teacher serves for your children as a model of upright and uplifting character, by all means express your appreciation to the teacher, but also make sure the school board understands how much it means to your family to have that kind of person in the classroom.

What I am suggesting here is that the guides to lead our nation out of the moral swamp do not all have to be generals in command of some nationwide movement. Repeated small acts by courageous and thoughtful people will often prime the pump, bringing forth a flow of similar acts by other citizens.

In undertaking to support that which is righteous and to express rational disapproval for that which is morally destructive, I think we need to understand as well as we can the paradox which governs human response to moral principle. For the religious person, the greatest freedom comes only with total commitment to God. Perhaps you are familiar with the poem by Francis Thompson, entitled "The Hound of Heaven." It is the story of one man's effort to seek pleasure and peace of mind apart from God. In his words:

> For, though I knew His love Who followed,
> Yet was I sore adread
> Lest, having Him, I must have naught beside.

This fear of being stifled and hemmed in by religious commitment, so powerfully described by Francis Thompson, is banished only in the discovery that it is precisely within such a commitment that life is fulfilled. There is, I believe, an analogy in our secular activities. Each group, be it family or friendship, college or business firm, city or nation, exists to accomplish certain functions. Trial and error and common sense eventually identify certain things which the members must do and must not do if the group is to hold together and be effective. Living in a household would be impossible if some member persisted in flooding the place by leaving the faucets on with the stopper closed, so the prohibition of that act becomes a rule of the household. Thus it is that codes of conduct suitable to each kind of group are developed.

The person who refuses to abide by the ground rules runs afoul of his colleagues, generates animosities, and must waste time and effort and burden his conscience with furtive activities to cover up his wrongdoing. By contrast, the person who learns and abides by the rules of the group, if they are reasonable and legitimate, is free to be creative within those limits. He is a welcome member of the group and is more likely to be productive as a result of that welcomeness.

The "sentiment of submission" as Duncan Williams has called it, is one of the most fundamental aspects of human life and one of the least understood today. The physicist understands that he cannot defy the laws of physics and amount to anything as a physicist. The religious person knows that he cannot ignore the dictates of his church and maintain his own respect for himself as a churchman. So, too, with the human being operating as a member of society. To disregard the tenets of courtesy, morality, truthfulness, kindness and the other norms of civilized living dehumanizes the individual; it makes him a social misfit and leads to loneliness and frustrations. Our failure to convey an understanding of this cause-and-effect has given rise to the tragedy of the counter-culture in whose ranks are innumerable young people who, like the protagonist of "The Hound of Heaven," foolishly suppose they can find joy and fulfillment by running away from the only source of those blessings, the commitment to noble causes and the submission to the obligations they entail.

In closing, I want to go back to where we began. The task that faces your generation is no less difficult than the work which confronted the pioneers of this state, but much of what they had to accomplish was starkly obligatory. For them to fail to take action often meant to perish. Not so today. There is no comparable sense of urgency upon us. It is so easy, even for the righteous person, to busy himself with the many real claims upon his daily life that he defers until some future time his involvement in the effort to clean up our morally polluted atmosphere and to strive for the health-giving and joy-bearing environment of respect for truth and principle and piety. Let me, therefore, make one request of you. I invite you to take a little card and put it on your mirror or fix it with a magnet to the refrigerator door, display it in some prominent place where it can serve as a daily reminder for yourself and a lesson for your children. I suggest you inscribe on that card the phrase, "Truth is outraged by silence." I earnestly believe that it has been the silence of the good people much more than the yammering of fools or the persuasion of intentional evil which has converted this once predominantly lawful and beneficent nation into a moral wasteland. That process can be reversed if enough citizens of moral conviction will raise their voices. I call upon you to join that chorus and prove yourselves worthy of your proud heritage.

May God be with you throughout your lives, and may you always be with God.

ENNOBLING OBLIGATIONS

YOU MAKE A LIFE BY WHAT YOU GIVE
By John A. Howard, Counselor, The Rockford Institute
Delivered at the Mount Holyoke College Sesquicentennial Program,
Chicago, Illinois, October 23, 1987

In 1933, *Within This Present*, a novel by Margaret Ayer Barnes, received the Pulitzer Prize. The story begins in 1914 in a spacious and elegant Lake Forest home where the family has gathered in honor of the grandmother's seventieth birthday. After the dessert was served, the birthday celebrant, Mrs. Sewall, startled everyone by standing up and announcing she was going to give a speech. "I thank God," she said, "that I can still feel young and uncertain and perplexed, yet undaunted, just as I did at sixteen. Of course I see a great many things in life that perplex me. And what perplexes me most is that I can't understand how they came to be there—in my life—in our lives, I mean. You see, we've changed. The family . . . We're not at all like what we started from. I've seen it happening for fifty years and still I don't understand it. We've gained some things, but we've lost others. On the whole, I think we've lost more than we've gained . . . We've lost the things I should have thought most likely to endure."

What had somehow been lost during the Sewall family's journey to wealth and high estate was the moral fiber, the indomitability, the spirit, which had brought an earlier generation as pioneers to Chicago and which had carried the senior Mrs. Sewall and her late husband through the loss of their home and their business in the Chicago fire. Those of us sufficiently seasoned to remember the good-humored spunk that was called forth among millions of American families during the Great Depression, are, like Mrs. Sewall, bewildered that the changes we have seen during our lifetime have included an apparent reduction in the dauntless determination to make things turn out OK, in the number of people who, in Mary Lyon's terms "will go where no one else will go and do what no one else will do." Puzzled by that lapse, we are grateful to Mount Holyoke for designing this sesquicentennial celebration to shed light on this shadowed corner of the American psyche.

Brian Griffin, speaks of "the ineluctable incandescence of the human spirit." He calls it "the mystery . . . the desire to be good. It is," he says, "the secret knowledge that only by being good can we become joyful." For many Americans of recent generations; the knowledge of that prerequisite of joy has remained all too secret. That isn't altogether surprising because there are so few efforts nowadays to kindle the moral spark among the young or even to let them know that such a thing exists.

In *The Closing of the American Mind*, Allan Bloom writes of the impact of what he sees as the contemporary university's moral agnosticism.

> The souls of young people are . . . spiritually unclad, unconnected, isolated, with no inherited or unconditional connection with anything or anyone. They can be anything they want to be, but they have no particular reason to want to be anything in particular. Not only are they free to decide their place, but they are also free to decide whether they will believe in God or be atheists . . . whether they will be straight or gay . . . and so on, endlessly. There is no necessity, no morality, no social pressure, no sacrifice to be made that militates going on, or turning away from any of these directions.

One hundred fifty years ago that was not the case, as the early documents of Mount Holyoke certify. An unpublished statement Mary Lyon wrote in 1835 to make known the nature of the proposed seminary concludes with the sentence, "We hope to redeem from waste a great amount of precious time—of noble intellect and moral power." The mobilization and transmission of moral power is clearly at the core of the educational design enunciated for the Mount Holyoke Seminary in the published bulletin of 1837. The text begins:

> This institution is established at South Hadley, Mass. It is to be principally devoted to the preparing of female teachers. At the same time, it will qualify ladies for other spheres of usefulness. The design is to give a solid, extensive, and well-balanced English education connected with that general improvement, that moral culture, and those enlarged views of duty, which will prepare young ladies to be *educators* of children and youth, rather than to fit them to be mere teachers, as the term has been technically applied.

Later in the booklet, there is an explanation that gifts raised by the institution will enable the students to attend at a relatively modest fee. That subsidy, "comes to them as a high and valuable testimonial of the estimate in which are held the services of female teachers, and though it imposes on them a debt of gratitude, it will be a debt which shall ennoble and elevate the soul—one, which can never be cancelled by gold and silver, but which demands a far richer return, even the consecration of time, talent and acquisitions to the cause of Christ."

As we know, the very concepts of right, wrong, good, evil, grandeur and degradation have been questioned and disparaged during the past century and a half, and have been largely drained of their moral force. Richard Neuhaus, in his landmark work, *The Naked Public Square*, has analyzed the moral paralysis that closes in on a society when religiously-grounded values are ruled off limits in the formal consideration of the issues that arise. Our concern here is the impact upon the individual human being of an ethos that rejects private virtue as a public good and grants supremacy to the refusal to pass judgment on individual behavior.

Let us return to that arresting comment of Brian Giffin's, "the secret knowledge that only by being good can we become joyful." I offer the hypothesis that the elusive and admirable spark within the human breast which we are examining today is only a unit of potential, which remains dormant and undeveloped until it is fertilized and animated by conscience. Spunk must be activated by a motive that subordinates the self to a larger calling. If life has no meaning beyond the fulfillment of one's own pleasures and inclinations, then there is no incentive to take the bold risks and make the sacrifices that concern us today. To activate that spirit, there must be what Duncan Williams has called the "sentiment of submission," the voluntary and ungrudging embrace of obligations to something larger and more important than the self. I would like to touch on several of the value-forming activities of our society which once served rather broadly to promulgate those ennobling obligations.

Let us begin with education. Of the innumerable analyses of the 1964 eruption at the Berkely campus, one of the most sensitive, and perhaps most accurate, was a pair of articles by Max Ways published in *Fortune* magazine. Ways perceived that for some reason the moral energies of the students were being channeled into activities which were essentially negative, activities which complained about and attacked the structures of American society rather than working within the system in the fulfillment of moral values. He anticipated by more than two decades Allan Bloom's insight of the damaging impact of the institutionalized openness to all points of view. The emphasis placed by the academy on refusing to pass judgment on the beliefs and behavior of anyone else had served to eliminate from the educational process the approval and advocacy of standards of conduct. Virtue had somehow been redefined to be personal prejudice. Virtue had, in fact, become disreputable. There was no grandeur to be found in individual behavior. As a consequence, the only acceptable moral causes were ones to straighten out wayward institutions or force a change in wrong-headed policies. In that philosophically restricted ethical environment, almost any self-styled guru who did proclaim that he knew the way to individual glory enlisted a following larger than the validity and persuasiveness of his cause would normally deliver. In retrospect, and in the light of the understanding provided by Max Ways, this student ferment was rightly designated a protest movement. Protest is a pretty thin gruel to nourish the spirit, but for many people of that generation, that was as close as they came to moral and ethical training during their college years.

I would like to share with you a passage from a letter which the novelist, Otis Carney, wrote several years ago about his attendance at an Ivy League college during World War II.

> What I would tell [my alma mater] now is that neither she (nor any other university of our era) seemed to train

> us for what we were inside. There is nothing in my education that addressed itself to the "not by bread alone" part of me—the miracle of the human spirit, and by this I don't necessarily mean spirit as expressed in religion, though that is part of it. I'm talking of Pope's "know thyself." Or Eliot's "teach us to care and not to care" . . . When Eliot said, "Teach us to care and not to care, what he seemed to be saying was: that we should care terribly about what we do in this world, hurl ourselves into it with all the intelligence and courage we can muster. And then we should not care about the reward. For, in truth, just our commitment, our energizing of our spirit in its noble connection to the struggle of all mankind—that has been our reward . . . Would that a student might emerge from [our university] convinced of the value of transcendence, for that is the only route to his completion."

A comparable failure on the part of contemporary American religious institutions was brought into sharp focus by a program at Rockford College in 1973. As part of a campus-wide consideration of American Indian culture, the author/professor N. Scott Momaday spoke of the nature and practice of his Navajo faith. He told of a ceremonial song that celebrated the wonders of nature. I quote from his speech:

> The singer stands at the center of sound, of motion, of life. Nothing within the whole sphere of being is inaccessible to him or lost upon him. At least we have the sense that this is so, and so does he. His song is full of reverence, of wonder and delight—and of confidence as well. He knows something about himself and the world in which he lives.
>
> And he knows that he knows. He is at peace.

At the conclusion of Dr. Momaday's speech, there was prolonged silence. Finally, there was a storm of applause. Seasoned observers knew that something extraordinary had taken place. The power of the audience response signaled much more than appreciation of a superb lecture. The speaker had struck a resonance deep within his listeners.

"Of reverence, of wonder and delight—and of confidence as well . . . He is at peace," said Momaday. Anyone who has worked with college students in recent years know that reverence, wonder, confidence and inner peace are rare in America's young people. Still, that infrequency doesn't necessarily signify an intentional rejection. Dr. Momaday had rendered mystery and awe and eternity, palpable and kindly, and the obligations of the participants in the Navajo faith were readily understood to be natural and benevolent, not burdens, not threats, not restrictions. And that message was warmly embraced, apparently an unfamiliar message for most of that audience.

The family, like education, religion and literature, also used to play a regular and important role in transmitting to each new generation an understanding that life requires of each person the shouldering of obligations and duties. The young learned within the home that the fulfillment of their responsibilities is not just the dues one pays for being part of a social group, but also provides both psychic and social benefits. It was the loss of this aspect of family life that Mrs. Sewall was lamenting at her 70th birthday dinner, the lapse of all those kindly, supportive, homely blessings.

Among those home-bestowed blessings are an unpretentious sense of self-worth and a hierarchy of values which buttress the individual against the disappointments and reversals of life. The Harvard research psychiatrist, Robert Coles, dwelt on the subject of suicide in a *Chicago Tribune* interview several months ago. "Many adolescent suicides we read about," he said, "make a statement about the kinds of lives these kids have been brought up to live. It is pathological narcissism at work. These kids haven't grown up with a sense that they have obligations. Acting out through suicide, is extreme self-centeredness, an attitude that has never been challenged by their parents or by their world. In fact, it may even be encouraged." Coles went on to emphasize that what leads children to self-destruction is not media attention to other youth suicides, but the "underlying festerings of self-centered, unchallenged, rootless lives."

Well, what does all this add up to? This perspective is offered from one whose educational career was bisected by the watershed era of the sixties. It is difficult for today's college personnel to imagine what it was like to participate in a pre-1960 academic community when the ancient standards of lawfulness, civility, morality, truthfulness, rational debate and respect for an opposing viewpoint still carried authority and provided unity and amity within the educational enterprise. The life of the academic community, like the life of the individual human being has been trivialized, and impoverished and rendered hollow and mean-spirited by the rejection of transcendent purpose and the cancellation of the civilized norms imposed by such purpose.

The very thought of identifying certain traits of character as desirable in all college graduates and seeking educational means to strengthen those ideals of human behavior is now anathema within the reigning academic orthodoxy. Therefore, any attempt to amend the educational system to train the student for a civilized and honorable life cannot direct itself to the substance of education, but must be restricted to procedural changes, truly an exercise in rearranging the deck chairs on the Titanic.

In our day too often we continue to graduate cultural orphans, who don't even have a nodding acquaintance with the visions of grandeur which shaped Western civilization, the ideals for which untold heroes and heroines of the past sacrificed that we might live in freedom today. Nor are those who did the sacrificing sufficiently known and understood to be perceived as desirable role models. Lacking comprehension, the graduates of our colleges are inclined to equate pleasure with joy. And they are disinclined to "go where no one else will go and do what no one else will do" because they do not know, indeed, no one has tried to help them understand, that although you make a living by what you get, you make a life by what you give.

It seems to me that high on the agenda for our colleges should be a plan to enlist the students as dedicated partisans of abiding, ennobling obligations.

CIVIC VIRTUE AND THE MODERN CITY

by
Dr. John A. Howard, President
The Rockford Institute
at a
Rockford Institute Dinner
Rockford, Illinois
May 14, 1986

On April 29, a radioactive cloud drifting over Scandinavia brought news of a catastrophe that had occurred in Soviet Russia. The meltdown of the power plant at Chernobyl spelled a frightful and devastating end to a system that was intended to bring light and fruitfulness to the Russian people.

Three months earlier, on January 25, the airwaves over North America brought news of a catastrophe in the United States, a catastrophe which in the loss of lives and destruction of property, makes the Chernobyl casualties seem paltry and insignificant. For Americans, too, there was a moment of truth as it became clear that miscalculations about a system intended to bring enlightenment and fulfillment had resulted in vast destruction. The Russian calamity was technological. It involved a single incident at one location. The American calamity is cultural. It pervades the nation and the damaging impact is a continuing process, not a passing event.

The revelation of America's troubles occurred on a CBS two-hour television special hosted by Bill Moyers. The title of the program was, "The Vanishing Family—Crisis in Black America." It revealed the way of life and the attitudes of young blacks in Newark, New Jersey, who are trapped in a sub-civilization that degrades and trivializes human beings. The importance, the abiding importance, of that television program was that it established the fact that what has rotted the fabric of inner-city life over the last twenty years is the collapse of America's primary value system.

The transcript of the television show identifies fixed patterns of harmful behavior. The inner-city young person tends to live according to impulse without any rational system of constraint or obligation, and expects other individuals to do the same. Drug-dealing, crime and homicide are accepted as part of life's routines. The young men have little inclination to accept responsibilities for a wife, a home or any children they may sire. They are caught in an institutionalized adolescence. The young women seem to accept their fate as sex partners and single-parent child-rearers, without complaint or self-pity. As was borne out in the TV interviews, this way of life is made possible and perpetuated by the programs of government support. The work disincentives of government welfare subsidies, combined with the failure of cultural systems to impart any understanding of or commitment to emotionally mature behavior, fixes these people in an endless cycle of generations living in a twilight zone of sub-human existence. It is of interest that recent studies by Charles Murray reveal that the same causes have produced a permanent white underclass in small cities as well as large ones.

There are, it seems to me, two important lessons to be learned from the Moyers' TV program. The first is that we have made a profound mistake in abandoning the moral and ethical values which sustained a remarkable level of civic virtue in the American colonies and which continued to give character and vitality to the American nation through its first century and a half. In the inner-city today where very few institutions effectively exert a civilizing and restraining influence, and where concentrated poverty aggravates all the most destructive consequences of the rejection of a cooperative value system, there has been a cultural meltdown. The damage is inflicted not only upon the residents and the property and the institutions of the inner-city, but it radiates poisons into the surrounding areas: crime, drugs, prostitution and mistrust of all strangers.

The second large lesson is that, contrary to what has been supposed, there cannot be any special strategies and programs that will alleviate the problems of inner-city populations. Their problems are not unique. The plight of the inner-city is nothing but the plight of the entire society in its most aggravated and concentrated form. Any successful remedial action will have to address the problems, generically, for the whole society. To the extent that a nationwide program brings relief, the inner-city people will benefit proportionately more than other people.

The point deserves illustration. For a long time, there has been a growing chorus of black columnists and black sociologists, black clergy and black civic leaders, all crying out that America must not tolerate the further destruction of the black family. They insist that we must move swiftly to help blacks rebuild a respect for marriage, a commitment to the traditional family. Those who join in this appeal include liberals and conservatives and progressives and people with no labels at all. They are simply black leaders who have eyes to see and hearts to care about the ever-worsening circumstances of inner-city life.

Are there ways to reestablish among inner-city blacks a new allegiance to the family norm wile the rest of the society keeps marching further away from that norm into the realms of sexual liberation and sexual aberration? Not likely. Listen to this interchange between Bill Moyers and a Detective Shahid Jackson of the Newark police force.

> Det. Jackson: You're born into a dead end. You know. And you're in that rut. If you're born into that cycle situation, how do you escape?
>
> Moyers: Why do they have kids so early? Why do these children have children? This is a dead end; that's a perfect description for it.
>
> Det. Jackson: Well, when I was growin' up, sex was almost a dirty word. Now, sex is what's happening. You know, they see sex on TV, sex in the movies, sex everywhere. And some girls think it's cute walking down the streets pregnant.

There is no way the family can be restored to a position of high respect among inner-city blacks while the national culture aggressively celebrates the sex-is-what's-happening laidback lifestyle. The catastrophe of the inner-city black family is the catastrophe of the whole concept of the family in America. The one cannot be repaired unless the other is, too.

It is not just black leaders who have come to recognize the pivotal role played by the family in determining the productive or destructive life course for the children. In the recently completed major study of street and youth gangs in our own city, the first item cited among the probable causes which lead to youth involvement in gangs and delinquent activity is the condition of the family.

> The family has always been the basic institution of society . . . It is there the child learns to love, to be loved, to work, to play and to worship. It is a place where the child is cared for and taught the value of getting along with people of all ages. However, the family has undergone a dramatic change. For all practical purposes, the nuclear family no longer exists . . . Traditional values, attitudes and skills are not being taught to many of our children in their homes.

Here is one other brief quotation from that same report.

> What do street/youth gangs do? Gangs pass on values, develop attitudes and skills required to achieve their primary purpose. They provide their members with the same advantages as do other "normal" groups. The major difference between joining a gang or a scout troop is one of values, attitudes and activities. Both groups meet the same basic human needs of belonging, acceptance, security and "being somebody." The scout troop will concentrate on developing constructive values, attitudes and skills, while the gang may shoplift, sell drugs, assault, and engage in numerous other criminal activities that relate to their purposes.

Values and attitudes, values and attitudes—the recurrent theme of the Moyers' documentary and the Rockford gang study, and the chorus favoring a strong black family. It would take a long time to list and describe all the headaches and the heartaches that bedevil the mayor of a modern city, but I think it a safe conjecture that a large majority of the most difficult and the most costly problems with which a mayor must deal, have their roots in this matter of destructive values and attitudes.

In times gone by there was a consensus of support among American citizens for a set of principles that defined civic virtue. Those principles specified what was right and what was wrong, and how a good citizen should behave. Patrick Henry, for example, wrote that he was guided through his life by a credo instilled in him by his uncle. It was, "To be true and just in all my dealings. To bear no malice or hatred in my heart. To keep my hands from picking and stealing. Not to covet other men's goods, but to learn and labor to get my own living, and to do my duty in that state of life into which it shall please God to call me."

I think that says it all rather nicely, but if you or I or Mayor McNamara were to take to the streets and the air waves to urge that the Patrick Henry credo be taught to all our young people in the schools and colleges, you know what would happen. First, many folks finding the vocabulary a little heavy, would suppose some character actor had escaped from a Shakespearean tragedy. But the big reaction would come from those who do understand, and who will be outraged that anyone should try to impose a single concept of right behavior on anyone else, much less on all our young people.

Here we are at the crux of the whole thing. Here we are, as I see it, at the fulcrum on which will balance the chance for building hope and civility and productiveness and dignity among inner-city residents or relegating them permanently to dismal, marginal living. Will the American culture permit the reestablishment of societal ideals of virtuous conduct and societal standards of right conduct and wrong conduct? At the present time, any suggestion that our nation should embrace a specific set of ideals and standards will provoke fear, anger and scorn rather than praise from the news media, the universities and, sad to say, even a number of religious bodies. Value-neutrality, or non-judgmentalism as it is called, sits in the seat of power in America's opinion-making activities.

This is not the occasion to review our progression from a society in which civic virtue had specific meaning and was embraced by a solid majority of Americans to a society wherein the very term "civic virtue" is regarded as an anachronism in the dominant culture. There is, however, one category of participants who have been so influential in bringing about the change and are so powerful in resisting a reversal that we need to understand their role.

There are certain professional groups which are the natural guardians and defenders of the political principles of the free society. Journalists of every political persuasion close ranks to prevent any narrowing of the interpretation of the First Amendment. So, too, do college and university professors when academic freedom is at issue. Any question bearing on the right to privacy will also bring a phalanx of defenders of that principle.

There are, however, occasions when the free exercise of one of those political principles causes a genuine problem for the society. When such a conflict does occur, it turns out to be a lopsided encounter and almost instantaneous victory. There is no effort to find a workable accommodation between two worthy and important concerns that have clashed. The defenders of the political principle rise in such numbers and with such indignation, that the people charged with safeguarding the community usually back way off and are reduced to nibbling at the edges of the problem.

For example, a number of state legislatures have tried to do something about pornography. The professional guardians of freedom of speech and freedom of the press have been so forcefully opposed to any restrictions on what may be printed that the pornography laws have usually ended up with only a tiny fragment of substance forbidding the enlistment of children under a stated age, perhaps 14 or 15, in the production of pornographic materials. The implication of such a restriction is that as soon as the kid has reached the specified age, he's fair game for pornographers. The legislators don't mean that, of course, but an endangered child is about the only thing that can withstand the impassioned lobby for freedom of speech and freedom of the press, and so the legislators hide behind the bibs of the little children.

You will recognize that any effort to reestablish the traditional family as the desirable pattern for life in our society is going to encounter more extensive and aggressive organized opposition than did the pornography laws. Even so, I am convinced that the family must be restored as the societal norm before we can realistically hope for progress in reconstituting standards of civic virtue. If within the family, as the most fundamental of human relationships, there is no pattern of commitment, cooperation and willing sacrifice, then it is naïve to suppose that self-disciplined civility and cooperation can be made the acceptable norm for strangers living together as fellow citizens. The family is where we must begin to reweave the fabric of a civilized, sensitive, helpful and amicable community.

The restoration of the family norm and of the moral code that sustains the family may seem too difficult a task. It did to Bill Moyers. He was talking to a Mrs. Wallace who, with her husband, runs a community center which serves the troubled people in downtown Newark. Listen to that conversation. I will conclude my remarks with it, because Mrs. Wallace says most eloquently what needs to be said.

> Moyers: You're worried about the black family. You think it's precarious.
>
> Mrs. Wallace: It's gonna be an endangered species.
>
> Moyers: Even though the messages that kids are getting from the society seem to say, "Do anything you want to," the United States Government, the government of New Jersey, a white man like Moyers can't step in and say to young black kids, "It's not right to have children out of wedlock; welfare needs to be changed; you've got to take responsibility." Who's going to say these things to these kids?
>
> Mrs. Wallace: Why can't you say it?
>
> Moyers: They won't listen to me.
>
> Mrs. Wallace: It doesn't make any difference; you gotta say it anyway. They may not listen to me, either. But I'm saying if you say it in your corner and I say it in my corner, and everybody is saying it, it's going to be like a drumbeat. But it's not just for me to talk about, it's for us all to talk about. And it's going to surpass [people's] color. And you're not going to be safe, and I'm not going to be safe unless we send out this drumbeat. Let's deal with it. Let's deal with the problem.

PATRIOTISM

Patriotism, also, was a casualty of the pervasive cultural change. Apart from the sports events which open with the National Anthem, and periodic news stories of casualties and military set-backs in the wars, love of country is a minor emotion in the lives of most Americans. George Washington, repeatedly stressed the need for the people of our free society to devote themselves publicly and privately to care for and sustain their nation and their free society.

The following is a montage of patriotic brief commentaries assembled to remind us of the deep commitment and pride and sacrifice Americans have poured into their beloved homeland through the years. The lives of Americans are impoverished by a luke-warm patriotism and the durability of the American nation is imperiled by dwindling patriotism.

I. Historical Perspective

In a well-functioning free society, love of country is the bond that unites the citizens in the common enterprise.

After King George III refused to act on the request from the Continental Congress to consider "the restoration of union and harmony between Great Britain and the colonies," a second Continental Congress was convened in May, 1775. Before the delegates assembled, fighting broke out in Massachusetts when Americans tried to prevent British troops from capturing military supplies stored in the towns of Lexington and Concord.

Anticipating war with Britain, the fifty-six delegates of the Continental Congress enacted a resolution of secrecy:

> Resolved, that every member of this Congress considers himself under the ties of virtue, honor and love of his country not to divulge directly or indirectly any matter . . . . debated in Congress . . . And that if any member shall violate this agreement, he shall be

> expelled from this Congress, and deemed an enemy to the liberties of America . . . and that every member signify his consent to this agreement by signing the same.[118]

The wisdom of those delegates in drawing up such a Resolution and pledging their virtue, honor and patriotism as guarantees of earnest support for the Resolution; and incorporating a provision of virtual exile for any who broke the pledge; and the fulfillment of the pledge by all fifty-six delegates; these amount to as noble a proof of wise and heart-deep patriotism among a deliberative political body as history offers.

A large part of George Washington's Inaugural Address thirteen years later was devoted to the one topic he judged most important for the survival and advancement of the new nation, the unselfish standards of behavior that will be required of the citizens. "Righteousness and Patriotism," he declared, "keep the acts of government just and fair and free from party politics, and they assure that national policy will be laid in the pure and unchanging principles of private morality."

Eight years later, in his Farewell Address, Washington, again, dwelt extensively on the character of the citizens.

> The name of American which belongs to you in your national capacity, must always exalt the just pride of Patriotism . . . Let me now . . . warn you in the most solemn manner against the baneful effects of the Spirit of Party. This Spirit, unfortunately, is inseparable from our nature . . . The alternate domination of one factor over another, sharpened by the spirit of revenge, natural to party dissension . . . the common and continuous mischief of [Party politics] is sufficient that it is in the interest and duty of a wise People to discourage and restrain it . . .
>
> Of all the dispositions and habits which lead to political prosperity, Religion and Morality are indispensable supports. In vain would that man claim

118 Worthington C. Ford, ed. Journal of the Continental Congress, 1774-89, Vol. III, pp. 342-3. (Washington DC Printing Office, 1904).

> the tribute of Patriotism, who labors to subvert those great pillars of human happiness.

Half a century later, President Andrew Jackson echoed Washington's plea to refrain from self-serving political dispute.

> The progress of the United States under our free and happy institutions has surpassed the most sanguine hopes of the Founders of the Republic . . . From the earliest ages of history to the present day, there have never been thirteen millions of people associated in one political body who enjoyed so much freedom and happiness as the people of these United States . . .
>
> You have no longer cause to fear danger from abroad . . . It is from within, among yourselves . . . from greed, corruption, from disappointed ambition, and inordinate thirst for power that factions will be formed and liberty endangered . . .
>
> Providence has showered on this favored land blessings without number and has chosen you as guardians of freedom, to preserve it for the benefit of the human race. May He who holds in His hands the destinies of nations . . . enable you with pure hearts and sleepless vigilance to guard and to defend until the end of time the great charge He has committed to your keeping.[119]

Although Jackson rejoiced in the happiness of the people, he felt moved to remind the citizens of their duty to refrain from political infighting in order to fulfill their patriotic duty to defend and perpetrate America's blessed free society.

Fast forward a century to September 20, 1945. The setting is Chungking, China where General A. C. Wedemeyer is hosting a dinner for eleven American soldiers just released from a Japanese prison camp at war's end. Years later General Wedemeyer reported what happened that evening after he had toasted his honored guests.

---

119 Messages and Papers of the Presidents, Bureau of National Literature, New York, 1897, p. 1526.

> General "Skinny" Wainwright, tall and gaunt, arose unsteadily to respond on behalf of his Comrades. He pulled from his shirt pocket a wrinkled piece of paper. There was silence. Clearing his throat, the old general read slowly. "Not for fame or reward, not for place or rank, not goaded by necessity, nor lured by ambition, my men suffered all, sacrificed all, dared all, and many died. A glorious victory was won, and we thank God and you for our freedom tonight.[120]

Seldom has pure patriotism been so earnestly and eloquently phrased, a totally unselfish devotion, a complete giving of one's self.

American patriotism is unique. In other nations, the people's love of country is inspired by a rich mix of cultural features uniquely their own—distinctive language, cuisine, beverages, clothing, folk heroes, literary, artistic and musical giants from centuries past, and architectural wonders known to every child—a mosaic of national treasures. By contrast, consider the fairly recent admission to the Union of Hawaii and Alaska. These two territories, culturally were remarkably different from each other and from the forty-eight states, and yet both were instantly accepted as full and equal partners. This welcoming embrace of peoples of a dissimilar heritage is a singular occurrence and reflects the extraordinary nature of our society.

The creation of the United States shattered existing concepts of political institutions. In a speech at Colonial Williamsburg, British Stateswoman Barbara Ward said, "The men who legislated here nearly two centuries ago . . . with breathtaking audacity stood up in this little room and dared to legislate for mankind. For, make no mistake, that is what they were doing. They do not say, "we Virginians," they do not say "we Americans," they say "all men." All men are free and independent, "all have certain rights; government ought to be constituted for the common benefit, protection and security of the people." Although she was referring to the Virginia Declaration of Rights adopted in June, 1776, these concepts were the principles enshrined in the Declaration of Independence a month later.

---

[120] From a 4/28/83 speech by General Wedemeyer to the China Burma, India Veterans Association sent to my by General Wedemeyer.

The compelling attraction of America for immigrants throughout the world was the assurance of liberty and equal justice for all. These features were governmental marvels beyond belief and never experienced in the rest of the world. And they still are for many new Americans. Here is a relatively current testimonial.

II. Testimonial of a New American Citizen "The New Freedom to Live a Dream" Abdul Rahmann Abdi Chicago Tribune July 4, 1991

The joy of today, when America celebrates the 215th anniversary of the Declaration of Independence, is not limited to those born here. Millions of immigrants who have come to the United States in search of the American dream will be amongst them. I am proud to be one of them.

Born poor in a little town, Jigjiga, in Western Somalia, I had little chance to succeed in life. In much of black Africa, opportunities are determined by the dictators and the massive bureaucracies that run countries—at gunpoint. Freedom of thought, of expression, of association and of religion are deemed to be diseases promoted by the subversive West. And economic opportunity—in a society in which the socialist government controls nearly all aspects of the economy—is limited to the few elite.

This is what led me to look for an escape to America.

On Dec. 27, 1983, after a decade of planning my trip, I arrived at JFK Airport in New York. As I saw the statue of Lady Liberty, the words "Give me your tired, your poor, your huddled masses yearning to breathe free" came to my mind, and tears flowed down my cheeks.

Much to my delight, I found America to be a country full of individuals with a strong belief in themselves, guided by the principle that each of us will fail or succeed in life by our own efforts, ambitions and dreams. I took this to heart and strove to become just like them. A new American. But unlike most of them, I did not have a good enough grasp of the language, the culture or the history of the New World to participate in the race for the American dream. I had a lot of catching up to do.

I enrolled in English courses at Montgomery County Community College in Maryland, where I met many students from Asia, South America and Africa. And in the evenings and on weekends, I worked at a McDonald's to make some money for tuition and books. Within two semesters I was taking math, history and English classes, this time with native Americans.

As I assimilated into the American culture and way of life, I couldn't help but be interested in the political discussions that surrounded the 1988 presidential campaign. Given my experience of living in a small country with a big government, I was drawn to the party of Ronald Reagan, and Abraham Lincoln before him, which stood for reducing the power of the state and increasing the opportunity of the individual and the family. When I began to advocate conservative values in the campus newspaper—low taxes, a strong national defense, support for democracy and free markets, educational vouchers, and punishment, not sympathy, for criminals—I made friends as well as adversaries. But this was my first exercise in a political discourse in a free society, where ideas are cherished, and I thrived on it.

I then began to think not only of my new freedoms, but of my new loyalties. On April 26, 1991, I sat in a Baltimore courtroom for my citizenship ceremony with 95 other immigrants to whom America had given a second lease on life. I couldn't help but notice tears flowing from the eyes of grown men with gray hair, whose breath was taken away by becoming citizens of a country they had come to love. I, too, wept openly.

This may sound odd to those of you who were born here, but this country really is a beacon of hope, to which the persecuted can turn. Every American school child knows their names—Washington, Jefferson, Hamilton, Madison and Franklin—but not everyone knows what they accomplished. Their democratic maxim, "that all men are created equal," has made America the hope of mankind.[121]

III. AMERICA'S PATRIOT PRESIDENT

Following the death of Ronald Reagan there was a spontaneous truce in the continuous media barrage of angry criticism hurled at President

[121] Chicago Tribune, July 4, 1991.

Bush and his Administration. For a week the news was dominated by fond memories and praise of another president. Although it was a time of mourning, the relief from the hostility of the political campaign, combined with the numerous stories of Ronald Reagan's courage, optimism, kindness and good humor made it a welcome period of national amity, and, for many, of renewed pride in their country.

There is an eternal human hunger for leaders who proclaim and champion ideals, who embody the principles undergirding those ideals, and who provide hope and inspiration to the people. During the two decades prior to the Reagan election, the sour cynicism about, and criticism of, America that prevailed in the media, academia and the entertainment industry cast a pall over patriotism and other idealistic sentiments. It became a modern Dark Age which James Reston in 1969, perceived as "a new pessimism," Arthur Burns as "a loss of faith in our institutions," and Archibald MacLeish, as "an anesthesia of the soul."

Suddenly America had a leader who reversed the engines. As Margaret Thatcher said: "Others prophesied the decline of the West; he inspired America and its allies with renewed faith in its mission of freedom. Others saw only limits to growth; he transformed a stagnant economy into an engine of opportunity. His politics had a freshness and optimism that won converts from every class and nation—and ultimately from the very heart of the evil empire."

One startling aspect of that freshness was the fact that he did not seek the presidency for fame or power or personal advancement. As he said in his speech to the nation when leaving office, "I never meant to go into politics . . . but I was raised to believe you had to pay your way for the blessings bestowed on you. I was happy with my career in the entertainment world, but I ultimately went into politics because I wanted to protect something precious." Serving his country was a natural and genuine motive and gave him the freedom to follow whatever course he judged best for the nation. Self-seeking moneyed pressure groups had no claim on him.

The something precious he wanted to protect was, naturally, the first point he made in his Farewell Speech. He spoke of an incident involving the Midway aircraft carrier in the China Sea. They spotted a small craft filled with "Boat People," trying to escape from Communist tyranny. As the launch from the Midway brought them back to the Carrier, a refugee shouted to a seaman way up on the deck, "Hello, American sailor. Hello,

Freedom Man." What more poignant illustration could there be to exemplify the preciousness of freedom to all human beings?

The religious up-bringing which instilled in him the duty to be of service to the community also taught him to serve and love other people. Vic President Cheney in his eulogy stated, "If Ronald Reagan ever uttered a cynical, or cruel, or selfish word, the moment went unrecorded." President Bush said, "Ronald Reagan carried himself, even in the most powerful office, with a decency and attention to small kindnesses that define a good life. He was a courtly, gentle and considerate man, never known to slight or embarrass others."

Ronald Reagan reawakened in our nation an appreciation of the depth and beneficent power of the basic ideals of our free society and labored to help other nations adopt and benefit from them.

A Patriot through and through and a great blessing for our nation!

IV. In Remembrance of D-Day by Ronald Reagan

History has proven that democracy is worth dying for because 'it's the most deeply honorable form of government ever devised by man.'

Following is an excerpt from a speech delivered by President Ronald Reagan at Pointe de Hoc in Normandy on June 6, 1984, the 40th anniversary of D-Day. Today is the 60th anniversary of the battle in Normandy, which foreshadowed the end of Hitler's dream of Nazi domination.

We're here to mark that day in history when the Allied peoples joined in battle to reclaim this continent to liberty. For four long years, much of Europe had been under a terrible shadow. Free nations had fallen, Jews cried out in the death-camps, millions cried out for liberation. Europe was enslaved, and the world prayed for its rescue. Here in Normandy the rescue began. Here the Allies stood and fought against tyranny in a giant undertaking unparalleled in human history.

We stand on a lonely, wind-swept point on the northern shore of France. The air is soft, but 40 years ago at this moment, the air was dense with smoke and the cries of men, and the air was filled with the crack of rifle fire and the roar of cannon. At dawn, on the morning of the 6th day of June 1944, 225 Rangers jumped off the British landing craft and ran to the bottom of these cliffs. Their mission was one of the most difficult and daring of the invasion: to climb these sheer and desolate cliffs and take out the enemy guns. The Allies had been told that some of the mightiest of these guns were here and they would be trained on the beaches to stop the Allied advance.

The Rangers looked up and saw the enemy soldiers—at the edge of the cliffs shooting down at them with machine guns and throwing grenades. And the American Rangers began to climb. They shot rope ladders over the face of these cliffs and began to pull themselves up. When one Ranger fell, another would take his place. When one rope was cut, a Ranger would grab another and begin his climb again. They climbed, shot back, and held their footing. Soon, one by one, the Rangers pulled themselves over the top, and in seizing the firm land at the top of these cliffs, they began to seize back the continent of Europe. Two hundred and twenty-five came here. After two days of fighting only 90 could still bear arms.

Behind me is a memorial that symbolizes the Ranger daggers that were thrust into the top of these cliffs. And before me are the men who put them there.

These are the boys of Pointe du Hoc. These are the men who took the cliffs. These are the champions who helped free a continent. These are the heroes who helped end a war.

Gentlemen, I look at you and I think of the words of Stephen Spender's poem. You are men who in your "lives fought for life . . . and left the vivid air signed with their honor." Forty summers have passed since the battle that you fought there. You were young the day you took these cliffs; some of you were hardly more than boys, with the deepest joys of life before you. Yet you risked everything here. Why? Why did you do it? What impelled you to put aside the instinct for self-preservation and risk your lives to take these cliffs? What inspired all the men of the armies that met here? We look at you, and somehow we know the answer. It was faith, and belief; it was loyalty and love.

The men of Normandy had faith that what they were doing was right, faith that they fought for all humanity, faith that a just God would grant them mercy on this beachhead or on the next. It was the deep knowledge—and pray God we have not lost it—that there is a profound moral difference between the use of force for liberation and the use of force for conquest. You were here to liberate, not to conquer, and so you and those others did not doubt your cause. And you were right not to doubt.

You all knew that some things are worth dying for. One's country is worthy dying for, and democracy is worth dying for, because it's the most deeply honorable form of government ever devised by man. All of you loved liberty. All of you were willing to fight tyranny, and you knew the people of your countries were behind you.

Daniel Marsh was an ordained minister who served very capably as the President of Boston University during the difficult years of the Great Depression and World War II.

He spent some years studying the great documents of American history and provided the historical background of each of them in a book published in 1970 entitled Unto The Generations. Each of the eight documents is presented with scriptural connotations.

The Mayflower Compact
The Declaration of Independence
The Constitution of the United States
Washington's Farewell Address
The Star-Spangled Banner
Lincoln's Second Inaugural Address
Woodrow Wilson's The Road Away From Revolution

General Douglas MacArthur's Address to his countrymen from the deck of the Battleship Missouri at the formal surrender of Japan

In his introduction he says

> May the youth of America . . . become familiar not only with the documents here presented, but also with the stories of how they came into being, of the immortal persons who composed them . . . and as Adlai Stevenson once said, "A patriotism that puts country ahead of self . . . the tranquil and steady dedication of a lifetime.

Rockford College

When I came to Rockford on February 1, 1960, it was a proud college with a devoted faculty, most of them women since it had been a women's college until 1952. A number of the professors were brilliant, respected scholars approaching retirement. The College had a chapter of Phi Beta Kappa.

A number of prominent local businessmen, five of them Dartmouth alumni, were trustees as were alumni from various cities. Most of the Trustees were devoted to the College, but largely, their involvement was fairly well restricted to finances, the physical plant, the selection of a President and other key officials and ceremonial events. Karl Williams, the Chairman of the Board, was a Godsend. A wise and cheerful man who had been Secretary of the American Bar Association. He had not imposed his views on previous presidents who apparently preferred to steer the ship themselves, but what an enormous help he was to me and my colleagues after he was invited in!

I said we were in the season of recruiting faculty for next fall, but our salary scale was so modest, it would be slim pickings for us. I asked for suggestions about possible major gifts. He said one large, family-owned Rockford corporation had a substantial foundation that was generous to many Rockford non-profit organizations but our College was not high on their list.

I telephoned that corporation the next morning, identified myself, and requested an appointment with the President. I could hear him say to the secretary, "Tell him I am much too busy!" I said to her, "I will call every week until there is a time when we can visit." I heard him say, "Oh let's get this over with. Tell him to come over now." I explained some of our plans to strengthen the College. After ten minutes he said, "Thank you very much for coming, I wish you well." I said, "Sir, You haven't listened to a word I've said." He blurted out, "People don't talk to me like that!" I said, "It's true, isn't it?" Then he burst out laughing and said "Yes, it's true. Start over."

I told him our salary range was so limited it will be very difficult for us to enlist talented professors, especially in economics where able advocates of the private enterprise system command fairly high pay. After a half hour I left with a pledge of $100,000, for salaries in the coming year and again for the following year and an invitation to come back for a visit after that.

The following are excerpts from my Inaugural Address. I had realized that the generation gap and the rock music culture would require some departures from the routines that had evolved in the hundred plus years at Rockford College and I sought to plant some seeds for a concept of education which would extend our vistas and our concerns beyond the ramifications of the individual courses out into the contentious culture and its ramifications for a student's life.

AN ACCOUNTABLE PURPOSE INAUGURAL ADDRESS

by
John A. Howard, President
Rockford College
April 30, 1960

We have witnessed the solemn rite of the academic procession, an inspiring spectacle, ancient and honored. Down this aisle have passed scores of delegates each bearing the regalia that marks his institution. They have gathered here this afternoon to join our students and trustees and faculty in a service of tribute. It is not a tribute to an individual for which they have come, nor is it a tribute to a college. The procession would have formed regardless of the individual to be inaugurated, and it would have marched whatever the name or the size or the age of the college. This ceremony honors the human arts of scholarship and teaching and learning. It glorifies the divine atom in man's nature that stirs him to build a bridge to the next island across the seas of ignorance and fear and distrust.

In our country we have cast off forms and rituals to such an extent that outside of church services, our encounters with pageantry have been largely reduced to the mere spectacle of the Rose Bowl or the presentation of the Academy Awards. We have prided ourselves on the excision of links with the past, perhaps under the misapprehension that in so doing we were but freeing ourselves from prejudice and out-moded ideas.

There are times, however, when the public acknowledgement of tradition is wholesome and inspirational. No man could stand here under these circumstances and experience mere personal gratification in the office with which he has been invested. The academic ceremony engraves onto his total consciousness the ineffable responsibility now his, to carry on the quest for knowledge and to contribute to the effectiveness of the process known as education.

That responsibility is even graver in an era when there is mounting pressure to provide more education without a comparable pressure delineating content or purpose. Education is taken for granted as a part of our culture. The necessity for education is too often given priority over its nature and its results.

In America, our academic culture is a mosaic, pieced together of bright and durable jewels of incredibly diverse origin. Like a mosaic, its effect is something altogether different from the native source of the particles, and like a mosaic, the ordering of its parts leaves something to be desired if left wholly to chance.

The American celebration of Christmas includes wreathes and trees, stockings by the chimney, Santa Claus and reindeer, a crèche, bright lights on the eaves, wassail, carols, mistletoe, greeting cards and the exchange of gifts. The source of each of these customs is almost forgotten. The relationship which each may once have had to the celebration of Christ's birth is lost in the routine celebration of the holiday season. The degree of religious emphasis depends on the individual, but the season is celebrated by Christian and skeptic alike.

There is, I believe, a parallel situation in the observance of the educational season, from September to June with time off for Christmas and Easter. We have inherited from a variety of sources many goals for education and many techniques for education. Those that have caught on have accumulated into an aggregate of practice which has its own momentum and moves along unchallenged and unquestioned by most of us.

The schools of America have been expected, variously, to transmit the knowledge of the ages, to hold at bay that old deluder, Satan, to insure good government by creating an informed citizenry, to protect the nation against class struggles by equalizing the conditions of men and to insure us against crime by instilling morality into our youth. Overlaid on these objectives of promoting the general welfare there has arisen a new scale of aims for education, those directed to the needs and development of the individual student. The schools have been asked to maximize the effectiveness of the individual mind by making it a storehouse of knowledge on the one hand and by training the separate mental skills of memory, judgment, observation, and reflection on the other. Social and emotional growth and vocational competence have also become accepted points of emphasis in the process of schooling.

Colleges and universities provide for their students experiences which bear on many or all of these purposes. Too rarely are priorities assigned to them. Too frequently each faculty member considers his own intellectual discipline justified in itself, with little concept of or concern for its relationship to the total educational program provided in the institution. The result is that in the absence of an accountable institutional purpose the educational experience of the student is not the sum of its parts.

A study made recently at a very respectable university revealed that students and faculty were interested in different results from the college education. The faculty placed greater emphasis on intellectual growth than did the students, and the positions were reversed in regard to social development and vocational preparation. The student who thus works at cross purposes with his professors encounters understandable difficulty in integrating the separate elements of his college experience and in justifying his attention to what is supposed to be the central activity of education, the acquisition of knowledge and skills. Lacking thirst, he only makes ripples on the surface of the Illyrian spring.

In *Little Dorrit*, Charles Dickens provides a deft illustration of the problem and the product which concern us. One of the characters, a Mr. Sparkler, was enormously impressed by Miss Fanny's allusions to Dante. Mr. Sparkler's education left something to be desired. His own recollection of the Italian poet was based on a picture rather than on the poetry and therefore he thought of Dante as "an eccentric man . . . who used to put leaves round his head and sit upon a stool, for some unaccountable purpose, outside the cathedral at Florence."

Mr. Sparkler at least had the wit to recognize that there must be a purpose for the leafy headgear, unaccountable as it was to him. Without a clearly defined purpose, an educational program mass-produces Mr. Sparklers who are only dimly aware of what they see and what they study. What they remember will be odds and ends impressed on their minds by some particularly congruous or particularly incongruous relationship. The laurel wreath, Dante, the stool and the cathedral will add up to eccentricity unless the artist's symbolism is clear. The student and the teacher must share a common purpose or the student will not go beyond surface impressions of what he encounters in class.

Plato observed that all men desire knowledge, but not all men desire the labor of learning. For any project that requires labor rather than good fortune in its fulfillment, an accountable purpose is a prime requisite. Without it, one must expect that students will rate social growth higher than other elements of the college experience. Actually the term "social growth," as many students interpret it, is little more than a happy rationalization for having a good time, and student motivation in that direction needs no support from the college staff.

On a national sale the mosaic of educational purpose is a jumble rather than a well-defined image.

There are, fortunately, a number of colleges and universities which have well-defined purposes resulting in a common bond among the faculty members and a shared goal between faculty and students. It is at these institutions that the students work up to the level of their mental capacities and from which they emerge well-educated and confident people.

Within this group of institutions the principal objective of one may be quite different from that of another. The significant feature is that there is one common accountable objective within the institution, recognized by all who are affiliated with it.

In Chancellor Kimpton's last annual report on the state of the University of Chicago, he avowed firmly and conclusively that the overriding consideration of that institution is the extension of the limits of man's knowledge, the pursuit of knowledge for the sake of knowledge.

This principle is one that has animated many of the great European universities for centuries. At the Sorbonne, one of the most notable professors of the Nineteenth Century phrased the same point in a memorable statement. Greeted with an ovation in class the day following his election to Parliament, he rebuked his students in these terms: "We come here to treat of pure, unmingled science, which is essentially impartial, disinterested and estranged from external occurrences, important or insignificant. Let us always maintain for learning this exclusive character."

It is a worthy concept and we honor Monsieur Guizot and Chancellor Kimpton for their devotion to it. It is at universities like theirs that scholarship flourishes and the limits of our knowledge are extended.

There are, however, other worthy missions for institutions of higher education. The classicist, Professor Whitney Oates, in an address last January, pointed out that it is pertinent to ask the question. "Knowledge for what?" His answer to his own question was knowledge for the benefit of mankind.

As I read the history of Rockford College and try to assess the particular genius of this institution, I am convinced that it is the concept of knowledge for the benefit of mankind that has animated our curriculum, that has been the distinguishing mark of our faculty, and that has led to the achievement of our students.

It is my purpose today to reaffirm that concept as the philosophical basis for our decisions and the unifying principle we seek to provide for our educational program.

In an effort to identify the conditions under which man may fulfill his nature, one is irresistibly reminded of the aspirations which President Roosevelt set forth when he was trying to prepare this nation for its fight against Nazi and Fascist absolutism. The four freedoms which he designated embodied his judgment of conditions essential to man's proper development, but man does not automatically respond to the favorable conditions of freedom from fear and want, freedom of speech and freedom to worship when they exist. A program of knowledge for the benefit of mankind must include a commitment both to extending the conditions favorable to man's development and to bringing about a responsible reaction to those conditions. I believe that we must match the four freedoms with four faiths, which actually are but one. The four are: faith in God as a supreme and omniscient being, faith in man's potential for goodness, faith in man's ability to make valid judgments and faith in the power of an individual to have an impact on the world around him.

Almost all of the independent colleges and universities of this country were established by one church group or another. Some of the earliest of these institutions were intended primarily to train men for the ministry. Others provided studies in a variety of fields, but in the beginning the students were predominantly members of the parent sect and the program was heavily weighted with religion.

During the present century the religious affiliation of many of these institutions has been reduced to an historical curiosity. God has been eased out of the campus place of honor, and, as has been indicated, we are sometimes not too sure of who or what now occupies that place. The transition from religiously committed to religiously indifferent institutions is partly a reflection of a society that has come to believe that success and prosperity are sufficient in themselves and that they result from our own efforts.

The debilitation of religion on campus is also due in part to the apotheosis of academic research. Wide credence is given to the idea that doubting is the only sound position for the true scholar. There is a taint attached to affirmation in academia. Faith is not an acceptable substitute for fact, and tradition obscures truth. Many conscientious people in our profession hold faith to be antithetical to the pursuit of truth, and their influence on college policy and on impressionable students is not inconsequential.

One other element in the campus divorce from the church is the result of a paradox of democracy. In this country each person is free to practice his own religion. Freedom of worship was the lure that attracted thousands of refugees whose religious faith brought them persecution in other lands. One might suppose that religious freedom would lead to widespread and unselfconscious manifestations of religion in the public as well as the private lives of the citizens. The reverse seems to have happened. We include the Almighty in our pledge of allegiance (a recent correction of a slight oversight), we inscribe "In God We Trust" on every coin, and yet we all but prohibit religious expression at public gatherings in order to safeguard the religious views of the individual. To make the nation safe for religion, we confine the practice of religion to the church building and we stunt its growth. A good many colleges have shared in this backward advance. We have protected the flower from the wind, but we have also obstructed the sunshine.

The independent colleges that have thus forfeited their birthright have discarded one of the basic elements that sets them apart from the public university where religious practices are curtailed by law or custom.

At Rockford College we affirm our abiding faith in one supreme and omniscient God. We commit ourselves to seek the way of the Lord in our decisions and in our actions. If any calling is in need of divine guidance, and divine love, it is that of the teacher. His profession is a presumptuous one, for he influences human lives for better or for worse, often more by his example than by his lectures. It is a callous man who lightly bears the responsibility for his effect upon his students.

Beyond our commitment to try to live in God's service, we pledge ourselves to encourage our students to take religion into their daily lives to an ever greater extent. I use the term encourage for we do not anticipate that every teacher will become a preacher or every class session a sermon, but we shall continue to increase the opportunities for our students to add to their understanding of the broad field of religion and of their own faith or denomination through formal and informal activities. Ultimately, however, the greatest contribution we could make to their faith would be to win their acceptance of service to mankind as the guiding principle in life.

This brings us to the second of the four faiths, man's potential for good, for we take as our definition of goodness in man the quality of rendering service.

We believe that everyone receives a spiritual satisfaction as well as a sense of psychological well-being and self-respect, when his acts serve a cause greater than himself. Skeptics may term this reaction enlightened self-interest, but even they recognize it as a human characteristic. We accept it as evidence of man's relationship with God, and as that element of man's makeup which brings him closer to God as it grows stronger. A life of service is the fulfillment of God's commandment, Love Thy Neighbor. It is the application of faith in God to the affairs of daily living.

The third faith to which we make affirmation is in man's power to make judgments. If you cannot believe in man's power to judge, any effort to serve others must be directed by whim, intuition or chance. Foolish, indeed, is the life or the venture so guided. Man's judgment is undeniably fallible, and yet judgment is required of us unendingly through our lives. We believe that, with a conscious reliance upon the best knowledge we can obtain, judgments leading to action are both necessary and justified in the cause of service. This statement may seem to be so self-evident that it amounts to nonsense, but it has a particular relevance to education.

The stress placed upon objectivity by many in our profession may be self-defeating. Objectivity, when it becomes an end in itself, leads to inactivity. The scholar can afford to deter judgment indefinitely as he seeks further knowledge, but the responsibilities that most students will face after graduation will not permit them a similar disinterest. The educational program characterized by an over-emphasis on man's fallibility and the incompleteness of our knowledge will graduate scholars, but in most other callings, the same people will become a race of Hamlets, doubtful and dilatory. We cannot afford to have our college graduates withholding judgments for the sake of scientific objectivity while people with less understanding of the world are making the decisions that govern our society.

It is the faith in man's judgment that gives both meaning and urgency to liberal arts studies, to the kind of program which Rockford College offers. The student has an opportunity, in fact a required opportunity, to obtain fundamental knowledge about man and how he functions, about what he has accomplished and failed to accomplish, about his hopes and fears, and about the various states and conditions of contemporary nations. He also learns about the physical constitution of the universe and its relationship to human life. In our complex society we are confronted with the necessity to make judgments bearing on all of these matters. The effectiveness of our service to mankind will depend in large measure on the range and accuracy of the knowledge upon which we must make judgments.

It will depend, also, on one other product of the curriculum, our skill in communication. However wise our judgments, if we are incapable of conveying them to others, they are of little use. This brings us to the fourth point, faith in man's power to have an impact on the world around him. As our population swells and becomes more urban and more industrialized, it is increasingly subject to a sense of anonymity, and to a feeling of the unimportance of the individual and of the futility of trying to change the currents of society.

A sense of anonymity leads to relaxation of personal standards of integrity and honesty, as a sense of futility leads to an indifference to matters of government and law. Even in the pragmatic view we cannot afford to let either attitude prevail. The spread of dishonesty and of political unconcern will inevitably cause all of us to suffer. In the affirmative program dictated by faith the individual *is* important and he *can* exert an effective influence.

The point needs no elaboration in this ceremony which brings to an end our celebration of the Jane Addams Centennial. That one dedicated woman could generate so many activities all directed to the benefit of mankind, that one slightly crippled, small town girl could inspire beggars and kings with the will to join her efforts, that one common citizen from northern Illinois could leave a name that stands as a symbol of service around the world, is full justification for our faith in the power of the individual.

Armed with faith—faith in God, faith in man's potential for goodness, faith in man's judgment when it is based on knowledge, and faith in the power of the individual to influence his fellow man, we commit ourselves to the education of young men and women in that knowledge which will lead to rich and satisfying lives directed to the service of mankind and of God. This, I pledge to you, will be the accountable purpose of Rockford College in the years ahead as it has been in the past.

ENROLLMENT

To increase our enrollment, another college president and I formed the Midwest College Council. We enlisted eight other regional colleges in a program that took all ten college presidents and their Directors of Admissions in the spring and fall to different eastern cities where we held two assemblies at large high schools in different corners of the city. One college president and one admissions director would speak at the assembly of students from a number of high schools, about college education in our region, and would answer questions. Then, each college was assigned to a classroom where interested students could learn details. This program lasted three years and was very beneficial for us.

Our admissions also benefited from a decision made by the College Board Testing Service to compile and distribute the names and addresses of African-American students who had taken the test. I wrote a letter to every student on the list and said that ours was a good college with a sound academic program and if they would like to attend a college where they would be treated like everyone else, they might care to consider Rockford. This attracted quite a number of very solid students.

MOVING DAY

Ground was broken for the new campus in 1961. Three years later enough new buildings had been completed that the time came to consolidate the college operation which had had the women students living in the downtown campus and the men on the new campus and some academic departments housed on each, and constant bussing back and forth.

The enormous demand for funds to pay for new construction left the college with a very tight operating budget. Several months before moving day I met with our Business Manager. "How can we possibly pay for the move?" I asked. He said that we will do it with volunteer labor and borrowed trucks. I said, "You must be out of your mind. Have you ever just moved your personal library to a new home? Think of transporting hundreds of thousands of books and furniture and desks and lab equipment." He said he had already signed up almost enough trucking firms and moving vans, all of them happy to provide Saturday labor as a contribution to the college.

The student and faculty work force was augmented by neighbors, alumni, boy scouts and many others. The Red Cross provided medical personnel at both ends of the journey and alumni provided breakfast and lunch.

Unbeknown to the College, the Student Newspaper provided photographers to cover the whole project and wrote and published a handsome eight and a half by eleven inch booklet, dedicated to Karl Williams who had been serving as Chairman of the Board for twenty-five years. It was entitled "August 15, 1964." It was filled with photos and commentary.

The Foreword by the student newspaper editor said:

> This is a story of change. It tells of the beginning of a new era and the end of another.
>
> This is the story of Rockford College on the move. It tells of 117 years of tradition left behind or transported to a new home.
>
> This story is told by students. The words and pictures were recorded by members of the staff of the student newspaper The Collegian.
>
> The story is written for students. It is aimed at today's Rockford College Community and at those who have gone this way before.

> But this story is written primarily for tomorrow—for the students who will enjoy the fruits but who will not remember the labors of SATURDAY, AUGUST 15, 1964.

Another student-initiated service project was a pamphlet for prospective students, entitled, "All Right! What's So Good About Rockford College?" Forty Rockford students were interviewed and each one told about his or her academic program, and the sports and campus activities in which they were involved. The home address and phone number of each student were listed so prospective students can reach them.

In the text, the subject headings were: Academics; Administration; Student Government; Social Life; Worship Services; and College Philosophy. Interspersed among these paragraphs were clever cartoons.

The conclusion asks, "WHO SAYS SO?" "WE SAY SO!" is the response followed by another cartoon.

The generous corporate grant allowed us to hire a number of bright, enthusiastic, imaginative faculty. Two of them, Arthur Adair, professor of Art and Knox Fowler, professor of theater proposed that we close down the academic program for a week and present a Festival of the Arts utilizing as many of our faculty as had expertise in some aspect of the festival theme, as well as guest lecturers, actors, musicians. The idea was welcomed by the faculty and our first festival took place in 1961. The theme was the medieval period. It was so successful, we conducted one devoted to The Italian Renaissance two years later.

The schedule opened with the first of several performances of a commedia del arte, <u>The Twins of Plautus</u>. Plautus. Irving Stone, the author of <u>The Agony and the Ecstasy</u>, lectured on Michelangelo. The Northwestern University Chamber Singers provided a madrigal program. Walter Chrysler provided six major Renaissance paintings by Tintoretto, Veronese, and Grinnacci. IBM lent us its collection of models of the inventions of da Vinci. Princeton Professor Coffin lectured on Renaissance Art. We had a pageant of Renaissance dances and Suzanne Block provided a concert of "<u>Renaissance</u>" songs and instrumental music. The Chicago Art Institute lent us Renaissance majolica ceramics. The J. Pierpont Morgan Library and the Newberry Library provided books and manuscripts. Mr. Frank Vanderlip of New York lent us seven large tapestries.

Rockford has a large number of residents of Italian descent. All of a sudden Rockford College became a feature of great interest to them.

Two years later, in 1965 our Festival Theme was "Creativity and the Negro." As we began signing up speakers and performers, each one was so enthusiastic, his or her acceptance almost automatically included the question, Have you signed up so and so? I'm sure I could enlist him or her.

The program began with a production of In White America with the New York City cast. The actors visited with our students until late into the night, as happened frequently thereafter.

We had an exhibit of primitive art from Africa and Melanesia lent by museums and collectors in New York City, Brooklyn and Philadelphia, and photographs by Gordon Parks, the Life Magazine photographer, lectures by composer Hale Smith, a lecture by John Hope Franklin, "Two Centuries in the Negro Appeal for Reason and Justice," a lecture by Saunders Redding of the Hampton Institute, a folk music recital by Joe Williams, a panel discussion on Creativity and Race presented by Actress Vinie Burroughs, playwrite Louis Peterson and Saunders Redding. The African dance troupe Olatunji and Company provided music and dance from Africa. There was a discussion of primitive art by Whitney Halstead and his staff from the Chicago Art Institute, Poetry Reading by Illinois Poet Laureate Gwendolyn Brooks, an evening of Music with folk singers Gary Davis and Josh White, with Bass player Bob Matthews. Lectures by Lerone Bennett, Jr., Senior Editor of Ebony Magazine and Hoyt Fuller, Editor of Negro Digest. A panel discussion by Brock Peters, actor, Vinie Burroughs, actress, Edwin Berry, Director of the Chicago Urban League, Northwestern Professor Raymond Mack and Cecil Partee, State Legislator.

Opera Singer William Warfield gave a concert and favored us with three encores. The festival concluded with a "cabaret" featuring Bobby Short, the entertainer at New York's Algonquin Hotel, and his trio. This, too, lasted a long time with conversations to follow. Once again a major segment of the Rockford Community became good friends of the College.

In 1972, our faculty voted to establish a monthly Forum series to bring noted national and international figures to speak. Attendance at the lectures was required of all students and faculty members. The lectures took place at ten o'clock on Wednesday and were followed by hour-long participation in assigned, discussion groups led by faculty members. Students whose program of studies were related to the speaker's topic were invited to lunch with the speaker in the President's Dining Room and at one o'clock the speaker was available in the Forest Cool Lounge to visit with anyone who showed up. Each year a committee of faculty and students selected a theme for the series.

The first year it was "Causes For Optimism." The lecturers included Illinois poet laureate Gwendolyn Brooks, Indianapolis Mayor, Richard Lugar who later served as Indiana's Senator, theologian Elton Trueblood, microbiologist René Dubos, patron of the arts Charles McWhorter, political scientist Martin Diamond, and my Opening Convocation Address.

CAUSES FOR OPTIMISM—LECTURE NO. 1

THE GLORY, JEST AND RIDDLE OF THE WORLD

by President Howard
September 13, 1972

The ventriloquist, Edgar Bergen, once asked his little friend, Charlie McCarthy, what he thought of the rising cost of living. Charlie thought for a minute and then replied, "Well, however high it goes, I want to keep on doing it." Any citizen looking at his family budget these days might regard Charlie's statement as an expression of unthinking optimism. At all events, optimism is the subject of the Forum Series which begins today and which inaugurates a commitment that I believe will be of some importance in the history of this college.

These lectures and discussions involving all students, faculty and administrative officers in joint consideration of matters of general interest will restore on this campus a wholesome aspect of college life that has been on the decline in the last decade. The friendly interaction that used to take place among the various college constituencies has largely been replaced by departmental loyalties. Furthermore, the theme chosen for these lectures and discussions gives us an opportunity to counteract one of the central lapses of contemporary culture—the preoccupation with human weakness and human error that has dominated art and literature and public thought in our time. There has been so much emphasis on man's difficulties and shortcomings that our society really has not given itself much of a chance to be hopeful about the future.

The consequences of this cultural negativism have been pervasive and profound. One such consequence was highlighted in a recent lecture to the West Virginia Medical Association by Dr. Dana Farnsworth, the

Harvard psychiatrist who gave our Charter Day Address last year. He observed that widespread drug abuse "is a symptom of a complex social malaise, an index of low morale and discontent, and a contributor to still further community disintegration." A number of us who serve with Dr. Farnsworth on the National Commission on Marihuana and Drug Abuse have come to the same conclusion, perceiving that a dominant cause of drug abuse is a generally pessimistic attitude on the part of the user.

The fact that college students constitute one of the groups most heavily involved in drug problems urges the state of public morale upon the attentions of educational planners. Thus, this series devoted to the causes of optimism is not without its practical importance in addition to the more abstract intellectual challenge which it offers.

In contemplating what I wished to say about this topic, a line from Alexander Pope came to mind as a helpful outline for my comments. In the Second Epistle of his almost endless Essay on Man, Pope labels mankind, "the glory, jest and riddle of the world." I want to consider with you each of the three parts of that assertion, beginning with the second—man as a jest.

Some months ago, while conversing with some college students, I asked what each one hoped to be doing ten years from now. The first to reply said he did not think there would be any ten years from now. A second echoed that dismal forecast. Asked the cause of their pessimism, they spoke at length about the rape of the environment, the unending conflict among nations, the threatening increase in population, the exploitation of one group by another, and the whole dreary catalogue of man's most obvious iniquities. These students had been steeped in the failure, frustration, foolishness and futility of man's performance, and seemed to have concluded that mankind is some sort of colossal joke that fate has played on itself. Professional literature and personal experience tell us that this general view of things is not uncommon among college students.

Now it is, perhaps, expectable that people who are culturally deprived or economically shortchanged should be unhappy about the world, closed in as they are by their circumstances. It is a different and in some ways more critical situation if bright young people who have been privileged to study for many years are beset with pessimism, for it is generally out of the latter group that leadership for almost all functions of society is drawn. Leadership requires psychological as well as technical competence. The leader without hope and enthusiasm is a contradiction in terms. He is attitudinally incompetent to guide others to their common goals. This is as true in the leadership of a family unit as it is for the leadership of a school or a service organization or a government. The parent who is a pessimist imposes an enduring handicap upon his children.

Therefore, it is encouraging that recent years have seen a growing number of analysts and theorists concerning themselves with the climate of the classroom and the impact of the learning experience upon the attitudes of the students. The summer issue of Daedalus, the distinguished journal of the American Academy of Arts and Sciences, is devoted to the topic of "Intellectuals and Change," as the preceding issue concerned itself with "Intellectuals and Tradition." In these pages, scholars from many cultures examine the relationship between professional thinkers and the operation of the general society. In one article entitled "Intellectuals Against Intellect," the Polish historian, Leszek Kolakowski, who was expelled from Warsaw University and now teaches at Oxford, puzzles over some current aberrations in intellectual activity which he perceives as self-defeating for intellectuals and destructive for society.

He says, "It is incontestable that intellectualism and the worship of reason are natural foes of the belief in tradition; the link is obvious, it is confirmed historically, and is logically clear. But it is also incontestable that we can scarcely imagine how certain essential values, indispensable for society, can effectively survive without some cult to surround the tradition." Later he observes that the intellectual whose ideal is the absolute equality of mankind must demand the destruction of culture. "If equality in every respect is the highest value, then the most important task of society is to press all people down to the level of its least enlightened parts." In his concluding paragraph he states, "Intellectuals are by no means called to govern the world. Their most important function is to maintain and to convey the accumulated stock of human spiritual culture as common stock."

Another article from the same publication, which concerns itself with the tendency on the part of the intellectual community to discredit the society as it exists, is written by Harvard sociologists, Seymour Martin Lipset and Richard B. Dobson, and is entitled, "The Intellectual as Critic and Rebel." These authors survey the history of American intellectuals, noting their frequent role in undermining public confidence in the institutions of society. They quote comments of leaders as far back as John Adams and Thomas Jefferson, who expressed uneasiness about the negative influence of intellectual critics. They further note that even Woodrow Wilson and John Kennedy, who were seen as compatriots of the intellectual community, found their efforts to lead the nation hindered by the skepticism of the intellectuals. Wilson is quoted as decrying the perennial misunderstanding between the men who act and the men who write.

Toward the end of their essay, Lipset and Dobson observe:

> It may be argued that the growth of critical intelligentsia disposed to support the "adversary culture" and reject the worth of dominant political and economic institutions is undermining the capacity of governing systems in modern society to maintain social equilibrium.

I suppose thoughtful people will agree that any social organization is likely to provide better service if it is disciplined by outside critics who urge it to find better answers for the changing equations of human society. However, it seems that even criticism can be overdone. It may be that as we approach universal higher education, we are facing an unanticipated negative consequence of that accomplishment. It is possible that those institutions which facilitate the work and the life of society will simply collapse if too great a portion of the population is trained through the educational process to be critics and rebels, and too small a portion trained to make society's institutions operate as effectively as possible. An organization, like a person, can be killed or emasculated by kindness, but it seems that it can also be rendered impotent by criticism and abuse.

I recognize that my comments thus far are not likely to induce the audience to break into carols of optimism. I do find a crumb of hopefulness in that a number of scholars are showing the self-confidence to raise such questions about their own role in society, but the pertinence of what has been said is rather to try to understand why many students are discouraged about the future and perceive mankind as a jest. In part, this attitude appears to be a natural consequence of the intellectual community performing one of its legitimate functions either too effectively or else without a sufficient countervailing force.

It is true that man does commit foolish and destructive acts, and probably always will. Man does have a genius for making a fool of himself, but that is only part of the story. Let us move on to another chapter—man as the glory of the world.

Several weeks ago I had the opportunity to visit with Herman Wouk, the author of the current best-seller, The Winds of War. Since he has concentrated his attentions for some years on the subject of war, I was particularly interested in asking him if he believed that man had reason to be optimistic about the future. He said, "Of course!" I asked why, and he said, "The past." He seemed to find that a sufficient response, assuming, I suppose, that if I did not understand what was comprehended in those two words, no amount of explaining would help. His answer reflects the same attitude expressed by Will and Ariel Durant in their remarkable little book, Lessons of History. After more than thirty years of writing works of history, they took time out to offer some observations about their profession. At the end of the book, they state:

> To those of us who study history, not merely as a warning reminder of man's follies and crimes, but also as an encouraging remembrance of generative souls, the past ceases to be a depressing chamber of horrors; it becomes a celestial city, a spacious country of the mind, wherein a thousand saints, statesmen, inventors, scientists, poets, artists, musicians, lovers and philosophers still live and speak, teach and carve and sing . . . If a man is fortunate he will, before he dies, gather up as much as he can of his civilized heritage and transmit it to his children. And to his final breath, he will be grateful for this inexhaustible legacy, knowing that it is our nourishing mother and our lasting life.

A perspective such as this raises the possibility that those among us who are cynics or misanthropes or people without hope are either culturally illiterate or else have somehow become twisted so they do not know how to recognize a glory when they see it. As Herman Wouk implied, the reservoirs of history and literature and art and religion are filled with instances of men and women who offer abiding cause for optimism, who have triumphed in the face of difficulties at least as grave and awesome as any of our day. Now this thought is not a new discovery that Herman Wouk and the Durants and a few other rarely perceptive minds have somehow chanced upon. On the contrary, the transmission to the youth of the heroic exploits and the glorious accomplishments of the past have been the stuff of education for all societies, primitive and advanced, down through the ages. It is only fairly recently that education has relegated this core material to a subordinate role.

This is not the time to try to unravel the threads of educational philosophy which comprise the present tangled web of curricular emphasis, but I do think it appropriate to register upon certain priorities among the youth which may stand in the way of a renewed interest in our cultural heritage, and which may obscure the causes for optimism which that heritage provides. If we wish to try to restore a balanced perspective, we need to be realistic about the difficulties that must be overcome. A generation gap poses one such barrier. If the young people, for whatever reasons, are not disposed to look to their elders for counsel and wisdom and clues to the mystery of life, then the living repositories of hope are foreclosed to them. Experience does have some messages for inexperience, and live narratives are often a more persuasive instrument than written accounts. Similarly, the preoccupation with the present, or a supposition that today is all-important, tends to cast a pall over the study of history. The members of the "now generation" by definition make history passé.

A third attitudinal obstacle is the emphasis upon finding one's self. While this is a worthy undertaking, it is, I believe, self-defeating if it discourages efforts to come to know other people, past and present, whose lives give meaning to our own and whose careers testify to the glories of a life lived with assurance and hope. Still another impediment to the search for optimism in the annals of the past is our tendency to be problem-oriented in our examination of everything. In our time, the first inclination seems to be to discover what is the matter with it, whatever it may be. How did it go astray? Whose fault is it? We seldom wonder how somebody did his work so well, or why a certain group of people has managed to avoid the difficulties that afflict so many others. On the scale of the old cliché about the bottle being half empty or half full, we are a half-empty society. The generation gap, the focus on the present, the concentration on self-knowledge, and problem-oriented thinking all tend to discourage the search for hopefulness in our past.

There are, however, two present circumstances which argue in behalf of that search. The first is the One Hundred Twenty-Fifth Anniversary of our own college. As a part of our anniversary observance, we are announcing today an essay contest, open to all students and active members of the college community, including the alumni. The subject matter of these essays is to be the biography of some person no longer living, who had a major influence in the development of this institution. There will be two first prizes of $125, one for a student and one for a non-student, and up to twenty-three additional prizes of $50 for every essay judged worthy of publication. Details of the contest are available at the Colman Library.

One cannot be intimately associated with an institution such as this without realizing that good luck alone cannot bring it into being and sustain it. The viability of a college is measured in terms of the vision, the persistence and the sacrifice of countless individuals who have placed the welfare of the college above their own self-interest. A few of these people have achieved great prominence through their good works here and elsewhere, each one a vibrant cause for optimism to all who would study them. I quote from Archibald MacLeish, whose mother served as president of Rockford College, his view of one of our alumni, Jane Addams.

> When a citizen in our time decides to intervene on his own behalf in the affairs of the world, he does not buy a house in the heart of his problem and go and live in it himself. He establishes a foundation and staffs it, not with ardent and ignorant amateurs, but with competent professionals directed by a board of experienced advisors. The result . . . is far more intelligent and efficient public service or social service or educational service than Jane Addams' generation would have thought possible. But the result, for the same reason, is <u>not</u> Hull House. Jane Addams was not engaged in social service in this sense. She was not working <u>for</u> her immigrants and her poor: she was committing herself <u>with</u> them to the common life.

In addition to the few out of our past who have become widely known, there are scores of others less well known who demonstrated such devotion and such high accomplishment as to be a lasting source of inspiration to those who will take the time to learn their history. The essay contest, I am convinced, offers a many-faceted cause for optimism to all who elect to participate.

The other occasion which can help to diminish the reluctance to engage in historical study is, of course, the Bicentennial of the Declaration of Independence. The musical show, "1776," provides an appealing invitation to reopen the book of American history. The individuals who had the fortitude to defy powerful Britain and the individuals who had the extraordinary human insight to create a Constitution for a new form of government that could endure for two centuries constitute a whole catalogue of causes for optimism.

Hope, like works of art, cannot bring joy to anyone if locked in a vault or filed away unexamined on a shelf. The past is available to us as sustenance in times of disappointment and despair, but it is only available on our initiative.

Now it is time to consider briefly man as a riddle.

There is something basic in human nature that responds to a riddle. The story of civilization is the tale of challenge and response. The small child takes delight in asking a riddle, and he takes even greater delight in confounding the person to whom he has put his puzzler. "Do you give up? Give up?," he persists. There is gratification in having learned the answer to a mystery. This is, I imagine, the principal moving force for the research scholars. Indeed, the inquiring mind is the sine qua non for every genuine student, the inquiring mind and the sheer joy of discovery. A college president once, when asked how many students there were in his college replied, "About one out of five." Perhaps one good test for identifying the students among the "pupil stations occupied" is the response of the individual to a riddle.

Mankind is as complex and variable a riddle as any that can be conceived. In the more confident days of the Victorian era, William Gilbert said in one of his light opera ditties, "Hands across and down the middle, life's about the only riddle that we shrink from giving up." The problem of our day, and the one to which this Forum Series is directed is that some people are giving up on that riddle. The pessimist denatures himself as a student and scholar. If he is convinced that his inquiries will only confirm his dim view of mankind, the purpose of his study is soured and the joy of learning deadened.

It seems to me that teacher and student have a joint obligation in investigating man and the other riddles of the universe, an obligation to try to assure a balance in the course of formal study, examining enough of man's deficiencies and dumbhead mistakes to avoid any arrogance on the part of the learner, and at the same time building a year by year accumulation of knowledge of the glorious things of which man is capable. The college graduate who is convinced that mankind is a mess and society hopeless is, I believe, the victim of unconscionably bad education, and part of the fault is his own.

The graduate of a worthy education will have to come to know his own sound reasons for the kind of optimism William Faulkner expressed when he received the Nobel Prize in 1950. His acceptance remarks concluded with the statement,

> It is easy enough to say that man is immortal simply because he will endure; that when the last ding-dong of doom has clanged and faded from the last worthless rock hanging tideless in the last red and dying evening, that even then there will still be one more sound: that of his puny inexhaustible voice, still talking. I refuse to accept this. I believe that man will not merely endure; he will prevail.

In anticipation of our January Interim theme, "The Indian—The First American," I want to offer one more quotation, this one drawn from the Prologue of N. Scott Momaday's book, The Way to Rainy Mountain, which is a poetic narrative of a great migration of the Kiowa Tribe.

> In the course of that long migration (the Kiowas) had come of age as a people. They had conceived a good idea of themselves; they had dared to imagine who they were . . .
>
> The journey is an evocation of three things in particular; a landscape that is incomparable, a time that is gone forever, and the human spirit which endures.

> The imaginative experience and the historical express equally the traditions of man's reality. Finally, then, the journey recalled is among other things the revelation of one way in which these traditions are conceived, developed and interfused in the human mind. There are on the way to Rainy Mountain many landmarks, many journeys in the one. From the beginning the migration of the Kiowas was an expression of the human spirit, and that expression is most truly made in terms of wonder and delight.

Education can, I believe, be thought of as just such a migration, helping the learners to come of age as a people, to conceive a good idea of themselves and to learn that the expression of the human spirit is most truly made in terms of wonder and delight. If education can move toward that ideal, it becomes its own abiding cause for optimism.

TRUSTEES

A decision had been made to build and relocate to a new campus before I arrived. Some pledges had been made for this undertaking amounting to a very small part of what had been estimated to be seventeen million dollars. [The actual cost was more than thirty million dollars] I advised the Trustees that the funds which might possibly be generated in the city of Rockford and from our alumni were unlikely to approach the amount needed. So we set about enlisting new Trustees who were wealthy, nationally prominent, and generous. Each time we enlisted one, it made it easier to recruit the next one.

Among the people whom we enlisted as Trustees who served for some period during my tenure were:

Shelby Cullum Davis, Former Ambassador to Switzerland
Leonard Dayton of the Dayton Store Family from Minneapolis
Rich DeVos, President of AMWAY
William Lane, President of Lane Industries
John Davis Lodge, Former Ambassador to Spain and Switzerland

Columbia University Albert Schweitzer Professor of Humanities, Robert Nisbet
George O'Neill, Jr., grandson of Abby Rockefeller
Lawrence Rogers, President of Taft Broadcasting System
Henry Regnery, Publisher
Donald Rumsfeld, later Secretary of Defense
Admiral James Stockdale
Judge Juanita Kidd Stout, Philadelphia
Dudley Swim, Chairman of Continental Airlines
Frank A. Vanderlip, Jr. of the New York National Bank Family
Robert Woodson, Founder and President of The National Center for
Neighborhood Enterprise

We had three board meetings each year, fall, winter and spring. For each meeting we sent each trustee a booklet of reports from the principal administrative officers several weeks before the meeting. Following the meeting the trustees would dine with faculty, or students, or alumni, in sequence.

STATEMENT OF PURPOSE OF ROCKFORD COLLEGE

It became evident in the early 60's that colleges were headed into a time of turbulence and I asked our Trustee Chairman if it might be advisable for us to develop a new Statement of Purpose since what was printed in our catalogue was a fairly standard self-description of a liberal arts college and I believe we would be better served by a more specific description of our aspirations. Over a period of several years the faculty, administration and trustees formulated the following statement.

> Many people had a hand in shaping the Rockford College Statement of Purpose—faculty, administration, and trustees—and it represents an ideal in which we believe and toward which we wish to work.
>
> The fundamental purpose of Rockford College is to provide an educational program which will assist

the student to develop the full use of his intellectual capabilities and to call into play his highest motives so that he may be a creative, courageous and constructive member of society.

The educational program presents, through formal studies, a broad range of theoretical knowledge, attempting to give the student an understanding of himself, of society, of the natural universe, and of the worlds of art and humanities. The College further includes in the learning experience a diversified program of activities permitting the student many informal opportunities to augment, test and apply the knowledge obtained in his studies.

The philosophy of the College is based upon these premises:

Man is a thinking and feeling being. Therefore the College seeks to confirm in each student a concern for truth, a respect for fact, the habit of inquiry, the practice of intellectual discipline, and the art of creative expression.

Man is a social being. Therefore, the College nurtures in the student a belief in the inherent dignity and worth of each individual. It seeks to help the student discover the attitudes and conduct which will lead him to exercise that integrity and responsibility which are vital to a free society and provide a basis for mutual trust among persons, communities and nations.

Man is a spiritual being. Therefore, the College proposes to each student the importance of finding significance in life in religious terms and the necessity of discovering a hierarchy of personal values to which he will commit himself.

Finally, Rockford College seeks to improve and refine the educational process so that its program will be valid and vital for each generation of students.

TRUSTEES' SPEAKER POLICY 1964

Last September the Communist Party of America sent letters to student organizations in the colleges and universities throughout the country requesting that students invite a representative of the Communist Party to speak at college forums. The Maddox House Committee at Rockford College decided to request such a speaker, but first consulted President Howard regarding college policy on Communist speakers. Dr. Howard referred the matter to the Board of Trustees for a policy decision, and subsequently the Maddox House Committee withdrew its request. Dr. Howard appointed an ad hoc committee composed of administrative officers, faculty, students, alumni and counselors to study the matter and present recommendations to the Board of Trustees at its November meeting. In November, the trustees referred the matter to its academic committee for further study. This committee met several times, once with the ad hoc committee, and presented a report at the meeting of the Board of Trustees on February 23rd. After five hours of deliberation a decision was reached, and the following trustee policy was presented by Mr. Williams at an all-college assembly on Monday, February 25th:

"The Board of Trustees of Rockford College, recognizing the freedom to weigh ideas as a condition essential to the conduct of a liberal arts education, affirms with one modification the practice which for many years has governed decisions about bringing speakers to campus.

The responsibility for judging whether a speaker proposed for any forum, including the classroom, will properly serve the objectives of that forum and of the College shall rest with the faculty member in charge of the class or serving as official adviser to the group sponsoring the speaker.

The one exception to this general policy shall be speakers whose platform purpose is the advancement of the political or philosophical tenets of communism. The Trustees charge the President of the College with the final determination as to whether a proposed speaker falls within this exception. Such prohibition shall in no way be interpreted as a restriction upon classroom study of communism, its history, its purposes and its techniques, which the Trustees consider to be an essential part of the College curriculum.

The exception to the general policy is established only after prolonged and searching deliberation. Because the propriety of sponsoring an advocate of communism at a collegiate institution may be argued with compelling reason either way, and because it is a question directly related to the fundamental purposes of the College, the trustees consider it their obligation to assume the responsibility for this decision.

The present issue poses one apparent conflict between two sets of fundamental objectives of the College: the search for truth, presupposing a willingness to entertain all ideas regardless of source, on the one hand, and, on the other, the support of particular moral and political ideas regarding the nature of man, resting upon the conviction that each man has intrinsic value which makes him worthy to be educated for his own sake.

In American society the two are not incompatible, except insofar as one claims the right to preempt the other. Communism, because it respects neither the moral integrity of the individual nor the demands of intellectual truth, and because it subordinates the person to the state and principle to expediency, negates the precise purposes of this college and thus makes it impossible for us to accept its spokesmen in our forums.

It would indeed be a denial of our dedication to the search for truth to invite here a communist speaker whose very philosophy advocates deceit as a matter of policy."

BICENTENNIAL

Rockford was officially designated a Bicentennial College and we flew the Bicentennial flag during the year. Dr. Gordon Ross, Chairman of our history department prepared a bibliography of books pertaining to the theme.

The President's Opening Convocation that year was entitled "Our Sacred Honor." Other speakers for the Bicentennial theme were:

> Dr. Esmond Wright, Director of the Institute for U.S. Studies and Professor of History at London University
>
> Dr. Merrill Jensen, Vilas Research Professor of History at the University of Wisconsin, Madison
>
> Dr. Marcus Cunliffe, Professor of American Studies, University of Sussex, England

> Dr. Alan Heimert, Professor and Chairman of English and American Literature and Language, Harvard University
>
> Professor Dean Rusk, Sibley Professor of International Law, University of Georgia and former Secretary of State
>
> Dr. Harvey Mansfield, Professor of Government, Harvard University
>
> Mr. Max Ways, member of Board of Editors, Fortune Magazine

Robert Nisbet, the Albert Schweitzer Professor of Humanities at Columbia University, received the Ingersoll Richard M. Weaver Award for Scholarly Letters in 1985. His speech in response to the Award was devoted to one fundamental principle that educators need to keep in mind as they develop and amend programs of education.

The following are excerpts of that Scholarly Address

> How do we account for the distinctive profusion of inventions of the West? Largely, I would suggest, through the West's strikingly different utilization of the past. From at least the 5th century B.C. in Athens down to the beginning of the 20th century we see a continuing civilization that reveres the past and respects it as a storehouse of treasures . . .
>
> In its fertility of inventions and in its creative use of the past, the West has led all other civilizations . . .
>
> But the 20th century has become, on the testimony of many, the century of rejection, the excoriation of the past, and in the name of the future, the favored haunt of charlatans in our midst. T.S. Eliot speaks of "disowning the past." The idea of progress has become distorted into a justification for ridicule of the past, in the vacuous name of the future . . .
>
> There is fresh evidence of the truth uttered by every great philosopher and artist and statesman that the past is vital to human consciousness and will be squandered only at peril.

In this age when the past is largely disowned and true generalists are in short supply, worthy academic institutions will need to redirect their scholarship away from the pedestrian studies of modernism and mine the rich annals of the great thinkers of bygone centuries. We close this book with a list of analytical titans whose works contributed substantially to the philosophy of education which served the American society exceedingly well over many centuries and which, in the aggregate, need to be utilized in laying the foundation upon which American schooling at all levels can be adapted to the needs of a free society.

1. Aristotle (384-322 B.C.)

   Of all the things I have mentioned, that which contributes most to the permanence of constitutions is the adaptation of education to the form of government.
2. Charles de Montesquieu (1689-1755)

   A democracy or other self-governing free society can only survive if the population is virtuous
3. Edmund Burke (1729-1777)

   Manners and customs are more important to civilization than laws
4. George Washington (1732-1799)

   Rectitude and morality will assure that national policy will be laid in the pure and immutable principles of private morality
5. François Guizot (1787-1874)

   A sound body, a righteous mind, and a virtuous character—these are what a good education must produce—This goal is invariable and universal
6. Alexis de Tocqueville (1805-1859)

   By their practice Americans show that they feel the urgent necessity to instill morality into democracy by means of religion. What they think of themselves in this respect enshrines a truth that should penetrate deep into the consciousness of every democratic nation.
7. Nicholas Murray Butler (1862-1947)

His 1921 President's Report to Columbia University Trustees was a powerful warning about the disastrous consequences which would result from Federalizing American education and removing its control from local communities.

8. Walter Lippmann (1889-1974)

   Modern education is based on a denial that it is necessary or desirable to transmit from generation to generation the religious and classical culture from the Western World . . . It abandons and neglects the whole classical heritage of the great works of great men . . . There is no common faith, no common body of moral and intellectual discipline . . . We insist that everyone must be educated, yet there is nothing in particular an educated man must know.

9. Buckminster Fuller (1895-1983)

   Competent leaders must be generalists who understand human nature and the basic institutions of a free society and their fundamental principles which govern what they can and cannot do.

10. Robert M. Hutchins (1899-1977)

    The aim of any democracy must be the common good. The exact opposite of a democracy is government by pressure groups.

11. Viktor Frankl (1905-1977)

    The individual for whom service to others comes naturally can survive severe, inhuman conditions better than other people.

FRENCH PREMIER FRANÇOIS GUIZOT ONCE ASKED SCHOLAR/STATESMAN JAMES RUSSELL LOWELL "HOW LONG WILL THE AMERICAN REPUBLIC ENDURE?" LOWELL REPLIED, "AS LONG AS THE IDEAS OF THE MEN WHO FOUNDED IT REMAIN DOMINANT."[122]

---

[122] Unto the Nations, Daniel L. Marsh, p 51, ARC. Incorporated

CPSIA information can be obtained at www.ICGtesting.com
Printed in the USA
LVOW060829220612

287141LV00003B/1/P

9 781462 718313